NAUTICA
THE SAPPHIRE CUBE

Bhavuk Gupta

NAUTICA
THE SAPPHIRE CUBE

Eleven puzzles. One cube. A world's last hope

by

Bhavuk Gupta

First Edition – 2025
Printed in India

ISBN: 978-93-5525-244-9

For permissions, inquiries, or author correspondence, please contact:
Email: puzztales.nautica@gmail.com
Instagram: @puzztales.nautica

For my family
who stood beside me when I needed them the most.
Your encouragement, your faith, and the values you instilled
have shaped every part of who I am today.

And a special mention to my daughter, Shanaya (Tia),
the heart of this story and its bravest voice.
You listened to my wildest tales, solved every hidden puzzle,
and in doing so, became the very magic this book is built
upon.

A Note Before You Begin

Welcome to a **PuzzTales** - a world where stories test your mind as much as they touch your heart.

Somewhere within these pages lie clues, patterns, and secrets waiting to be solved. Will you find them?

Contents

Prologue - The God of Wishes

Once upon a time, a small village sat quietly beside the river Kharkhania - a river so clear it looked like liquid glass beneath the sun. People said its waters could heal wounds and carry songs from the gods themselves.

The village, called *Bistaria,* was a paradise of green meadows and laughing voices. Several villagers lived as one family. Their cottages bloomed with flowers, their gardens overflowed with fruit, and each morning they fetched water from Kharkhania, believing it brought them strength and wisdom.

Children played by the river, building sand castles shaped like the creatures from old stories. The air was full of birdsong and the soft rustle of leaves as the wind danced through the trees.

But sometimes, just before sunrise, when mist curled over the water, the river's song changed. One strange note would rise - gentle and sad - as if the river was trying to remember something it had lost long ago.

The elders said it was only the wind. The children weren't so sure. Some mornings they stood still, listening, their reflections rippling beside them - until the sun rose and the strange note faded, leaving the river shining as though nothing had ever changed.

And so, life went on in Bistaria - bright, peaceful, and unknowing.

For now !!!

The chief of the village, Bhavam, was kind-hearted, intelligent, and strong. He carried the wisdom of his ancestors and guided his people with fairness and compassion. His broad shoulders bore responsibility with ease, and his deep eyes held the secrets of generations past.

Though a warrior at heart, he rarely raised his voice - his presence alone commanded respect. Yet Bhavam had one weakness: he was deeply emotional.

At times, his feelings overwhelmed him, and he would quietly retreat to his alone place until he regained control. This made the villagers love him even more, for they saw not just a leader, but a man with a tender heart.

Bhavam was married at a very young age to the most beautiful girl from all the nearby villages. Her name was Rivaaya, and she was the embodiment of beauty and intelligence. Her long, flowing hair was said to capture the colours of the morning sun, and her eyes, a deep shade of emerald, sparkled with wisdom.

But her beauty was only a fraction of what made her extraordinary. She was a brilliant thinker, solving the most complex problems with ease, and her kindness knew no bounds. She taught the villagers to read the stars, to predict the weather by observing the animals, and to heal wounds with the magic of nature.

Together, Bhavam and Rivaaya were the perfect balance-strength and wisdom, power and grace.

And though peace reigned in Bistaria, Bhavam often dreamed of golden light beneath the river, of wings breaking through the water's skin. Rivaaya would smile at his tales, but deep down, she too felt that Kharkhania was waiting-for them.

One day, Bhavam and Rivaaya were walking along the banks of the Kharkhania River when they saw something unusual. The calm sound of the waves hitting the rocks was broken by a cry for help.

A magnificent creature, unlike anything they had ever seen, was caught in a fisherman's net. Its shining scales had started to lose their glow from tiredness. Without thinking twice, they ran to help it.

Bhavam used his immense strength to pull apart the thick knots, while Rivaaya soothed the creature with gentle murmurs. The river itself seemed to sense their determination, as the waves calmed to assist them.

With one final tug, the net came loose and the creature was free. It turned toward Bhavam and Rivaaya, its eyes filled with quiet gratitude. A faint glow spread along its body, growing brighter with each heartbeat. It stretched its radiant wings, and as it did, a burst of golden light illuminated the entire sky.

In that moment, time stood still. The wind ceased to blow, the river halted its course, and the world seemed to pause. Only Bhavam, Rivaaya, and the creature could move, as the sky above them turned into a swirling canvas of brilliant colours.

The creature, now glowing with divine radiance, revealed itself to be the God of Wishes. He spoke in a voice that resonated through the very fabric of existence, filled with gratitude and warmth.
"For your kindness and bravery, I grant you a wish."

Bhavam and Rivaaya exchanged a glance, their hearts speaking the same desire. They had always longed for something beyond riches or power-something that would bring true fulfilment to their lives. Without hesitation, they spoke in unison:

"We wish for a daughter."

"Granted," said the God of Wishes, and with that, he vanished into a mist of golden sparkles.

Time resumed its flow-the river gushed forward as if nothing had happened, and the sky returned to its serene blue.

Bhavam and Rivaaya looked at each other, wondering if it had all been a dream. Yet deep in their hearts, they knew otherwise. Their wish had been heard-and soon, it would come true.

****

Chapter 1 - When the River chose

In the months that followed, joy filled the home of Bhavam and Rivaaya, the beloved chief and healer of Bistaria. Their wish to the God of Wishes had been granted - a daughter. They named her **Tiara**.

She was the most enchanting child ever born in Bistaria. Her tiny fingers curled with strength; her eyes shimmered a mesmerizing shade of deep blue - like the river Kharkhania that had blessed her existence. A small, crescent-shaped birthmark adorned her forehead, glowing softly whenever she giggled.

From the moment she opened her eyes, it was clear - Tiara was no ordinary child. She was a gift from the God of Wishes, born with powers yet unknown - powers that would remain dormant until destiny demanded their awakening.

The Girl by the River

As Tiara grew, her laughter became the melody of Bistaria. She spent her early years by the edge of Kharkhania, chasing dragonflies, building sand castles, and listening to the river's whispers.

The villagers adored her. "Kharkhania laughs with her," Bhavam often said, half in jest, though his eyes would soften with quiet belief.

From the time she could walk, Tiara was curious beyond measure - always wandering into the woods, observing the play of light through leaves, asking questions no one could answer. "You'll chase the edge of the world one day," Rivaaya would tease.

"Then I'll bring the edge home," Tiara would reply with a smile.

Even as a child, animals were drawn to her. Deer nuzzled her gently, birds perched on her shoulders, and even the shyest creatures emerged when she was near. Like her father, she carried an unbreakable spirit, and like her mother, she possessed a wisdom far beyond her years.

Tiara's world was small, peaceful, and pure - untouched by darkness. The words fear and loss meant little to her. But beneath the calm surface of Kharkhania, destiny was already stirring.

A Storm and a Companion

On Tiara's fourth birthday, a fierce thunderstorm swept across the land - one stronger than the villagers had ever seen. When dawn broke, Bhavam and Rivaaya walked along the riverbank to find the shore littered with silver leaves and fragments of strange coral.

Then they saw it - a trembling, water-soaked creature washed ashore. An alpaca, small and shivering, with fur that glimmered like dew even in sunlight.

Rivaaya lifted the trembling creature gently. The river around it began to glow faintly, ripples forming spirals of silver light. "This one isn't just from the river," she whispered. "It's made of it." Bhavam looked closer, awe filling his eyes. "Then the river has sent him - for her."

That evening, when Tiara first saw the alpaca, her heart swelled with wonder. It bounded toward her playfully, its eyes reflecting both innocence and mystery. She named him **Teksh**, meaning *Light of the River.*

From that day, Tiara and Teksh were inseparable - bound by something deeper than friendship, as though the same current of magic ran through both their souls.

Growing Together

The years that followed were gentle ones. Tiara grew from a bright-eyed girl into a radiant seven-year-old - fearless, kind, and endlessly curious. Teksh grew alongside her, transforming from a timid orphan into a strong young alpaca, always at her side.

She treated him like a brother - feeding him, keeping him warm, and protecting him from harm. In return, Teksh never left her side. Wherever Tiara wandered, Teksh followed; whatever Tiara did, Teksh mirrored with playful grace.

Together, they explored every inch of Bistaria - the whispering meadows, the forests humming with life, the shimmering banks of Kharkhania. Villagers often said the two understood each other better than any human pair could.

And sometimes, when the sun dipped low and the air turned gold, they would sit by the river - Tiara humming softly while Teksh rested his head on her lap. In those moments, the world seemed perfect.

The Gift Within

But Tiara carried something even more extraordinary than her laughter or courage - a mind as sharp as crystal. Since childhood, she could unravel the mysteries hidden in nature. She saw patterns in raindrops, riddles in the rustling of leaves, and clues in the songs of birds.

Whether tracing footprints through the forest or deciphering symbols on ancient stones, Tiara's mind worked like a living puzzle - ever curious, ever searching. It was a gift from the God of Wishes himself.

Sometimes, she would whisper her discoveries to Teksh, and though he could not speak then, his deep brown eyes seemed to understand every word.

Together, they solved small mysteries of the village - missing objects, strange weather signs, odd markings by the river. Each mystery deepened their bond.

Teksh - The Light of the River

As Teksh grew, he absorbed the best of Tiara and her family. From Bhavam, he learned strength - capable of moving boulders thrice his size. From Rivaaya, he learned calm wisdom - an almost human-like understanding of emotion and pattern. And from Tiara, he inherited a fearless heart and boundless curiosity.

Over the years, something miraculous began to unfold. Teksh understood far more than anyone imagined - tilting his head at Tiara's words, replying with soft hums or short, raspy sounds. At times of deep emotion, he managed a few simple words that made Tiara's eyes widen with joy. He couldn't truly speak like humans, but he could communicate - through sounds, gestures, and the quiet language only she understood.

Yet, even as he grew powerful, he remained endearingly clumsy. He never quite learned how to stop once he started running - crashing into haystacks, barrels, and even cottage walls. The villagers laughed, Tiara sighed, and Teksh would bounce up, grinning sheepishly as if he meant to do it all along.

But beneath his playfulness lay something no one understood - a deep sensitivity to old magic. When ancient runes stirred beneath the earth or forgotten symbols glowed, Teksh's heart would race. The villagers joked that he could "smell old stories." Only Tiara knew it wasn't a joke.

His strength, intelligence, and instincts grew with time. He could swim through Kharkhania faster than the dolphins, hear whispers carried by the wind, and sense hidden magic in the air. And whenever Tiara faced a mystery, Teksh was always there - her strength when she faltered, her calm when fear whispered.

One Heart, Two Souls

Together, Tiara and Teksh became the living spirit of Bistaria - symbols of love, courage, and the harmony between humans and magic.

When Tiara was troubled, Teksh nuzzled her gently. When she was joyous, he leaped beside her. They were opposites in form, but identical in heart - the moon and its reflection, the river and its light.

Little did they know, their unbreakable bond was not merely friendship - it was destiny's preparation. For far beneath the calm surface of Kharkhania, something ancient had begun to stir.

The winds whispered warnings, and the river's song grew restless. And as the twilight deepened over Bistaria, the first shadow of a faraway world began to fall upon theirs.

****

Chapter 2 – The Arrival of Zarkasur

It was a bright and peaceful afternoon in Bistaria. The golden sun spread a warm light across the land, and the gentle waves of Kharkhania sparkled like blue gems. Tiara and Teksh lay on the soft grass near the riverbank, enjoying the cool breeze. They listened to the chirping of birds and the soft rustle of leaves. The world felt calm and quiet-free from any worry.

Then, suddenly-BOOM!

A loud roar echoed from the far end of Kharkhania, shaking the ground beneath them. The clear blue sky turned into a deep, frightening red, as if burning with hidden fire. The bright turquoise water of the magical river turned black, losing its glow.

Peace vanished in an instant-birds cried out in fear, animals ran into the forest, and fish jumped out of the dark water, desperate to escape. Then came a deep, heavy silence that covered everything.

A colossal shadow stretched across the sky, growing larger, darker, until a towering figure emerged from the hell. No creature in Bistaria-or even in the wildest of bedtime tales-had ever looked like this.

It was strange, otherworldly, a presence that made the air shiver.

Its head glowed softly, guarding secrets beyond mortal understanding. Its eyes glowed with red sparks, watching the world with a cold intelligence. The beast's body was broad and powerful, its chest covered in black, gleaming armor that seemed to swallow light. Huge wings spread wide, casting shadows over the land as if the sun itself had been hidden.

The wind howled as the shadow hovered above Kharkhania, the river trembling beneath its weight.

Tiara and Teksh could only stare-frozen between fear and wonder. This was no ordinary being. It was a conqueror from beyond the stars.

And it had come for them.

The people of Bistaria stood huddled near the banks of Kharkhania, their eyes wide with terror, their hands clutching one another for comfort. The sky, once bright and peaceful, now burned with hues of fiery red.

The magical river-their lifeline-no longer gleamed in turquoise hues.

A deep sense of unease spread through the village like a slow-moving storm.

The monstrous figure still loomed in the distance-motionless and silent, as if watching, waiting. It neither attacked nor spoke.

The villagers slowly returned to their routines, but every sound made them flinch, and every shadow felt too long. Life in Bistaria had not stopped-but it no longer felt alive.

On the third day, the temple bell failed to ring at dawn. Its rope had frayed overnight, though no one had touched it. The silence that followed felt heavier than the toll itself, and even the birds stopped answering one another's calls.

By the sixth day, the crops near Kharkhania began to weaken. The once-emerald leaves dulled to grey. The river still flowed, but its light had waned; when children filled their pots, the water no longer glowed against their palms. Even the wise turtles stopped surfacing.

One evening, a small boy burst into tears by the riverbank. The wooden toy boat his father had carved-one that had always floated upright-tipped over and sank.

Each sunrise grew quieter than the last. The air itself seemed to tire of breathing.

Yet the figure remained, motionless and watchful- an eerie guardian of impending doom.

He did not need to strike. Fear was his first weapon- and his favourite.

Every tremor, every prayer, every sleepless night fed him. The monster drew strength not from blood or flame, but from dread itself.

The more the people of Bistaria cowered beneath his shadow, the more his essence awakened in the void beyond. He was patient, letting terror settle deep into their hearts like roots in wet soil.

Only when fear ripened into despair would his awakening be complete - and then, through that dark harvest, he would drink from the world's magic as easily as a storm drink from the sea.

Tiara and Teksh could not rest. Their young minds refused to accept this as mere fate. They spent every waking moment trying to decipher the meaning of its arrival, determined to understand its purpose before it was too late. They observed it from different angles, sketched its terrifying features, studied ancient scrolls passed down by the elders, and even tried to speak to it, calling out into the void, hoping for a response. But the creature did not move. It did not blink. It did nothing.

Yet Tiara knew, this silence was not peace. It was the calm before a storm unlike any other.

Then, one fateful night, it happened.

Tiara bolted upright in bed, gasping. A sharp pain burned on her forehead. She clutched it instinctively, only to feel a warm, sticky liquid trickling down her skin. Her crescent birthmark was bleeding blue liquid. It was her magical powers.

A chill ran down her spine.

Teksh, who had been curled up beside her, sensed her distress and leaped to his feet. His eyes, deep pools of loyalty, met hers. He did not need to ask-he knew something was terribly wrong. Without a word, the two rushed toward the river, the cold night air whipping against their faces. The village slept soundly, unaware of the nightmare that was about to unfold.

The moment they reached the riverbank; a suffocating force filled the air. The wind howled as if it carried voices of lost souls. The river, once still in its cursed darkness, began to ripple violently.

Then, the creature's eyes snapped open.

Two deep, glowing red orbs pierced through the darkness, brimming with malicious power. They were not just eyes; they were endless voids of destruction, swirling with ancient rage and profound wisdom. A force so powerful surged through the air that Tiara and Teksh staggered back. The ground trembled beneath them.

Then came the voice.

A sound so deep, so thunderous, that it seemed to rise from the very core of the earth. It was not just heard-it was felt, vibrating through their bones, rattling the very essence of their souls.

"I am Zarkasur, King of the dark world of Sakaria!"

The words crashed into the land like a thousand storms, echoing across the sky, waking every soul in Bistaria. One by one, doors creaked open, fearful eyes peering into the night, witnessing a horror they had hoped was long forgotten.

"I have come to claim all the magic from this world!"

The river roared, its dark waves rising unnaturally high. The trees twisted as if writhing in agony. The air grew heavy, pressing down on everything with a force that made it hard to breathe.

"I will use that magic to empower my dark creatures…. To make them stronger…. So that I will rule the entire universe!"

A monstrous, ear-splitting laughter followed, shaking the heavens. It was not a laugh of joy-it was a declaration of dominance, a sound that promised the end of all light.

Tiara's heart pounded against her chest. Tiara felt tiny, yet she refused to hide. Teksh stood firm beside her, his muscles tense, his eyes burning with determination. Fear clawed at them, but something stronger rose within them-a fire that refused to be extinguished.

This was it.

The battle for Bistaria had begun !!!

****

Chapter 3 – The Cave of Two Doors (Puzzle I)

The next morning, Tiara and Teksh sat quietly by the dimming river, their faces shadowed with worry. The once-bright Kharkhania had lost its glow, its waters swirling dark and restless.

"We can't let this happen," Tiara says. "If Bistaria loses its magic, everything will stop-every song, every heartbeat."

Teksh nodded silently, his fur dull under the fading light. The blue glow from Tiara's forehead still trickled softly, the magic draining from her like sand through glass. Panic stirred in Teksh's chest. He had to find a way to stop it-fast. He couldn't watch his best friend, the heart of Bistaria, fade away before his eyes.

Then Teksh remembered - a moment from long ago, when he and Tiara had wandered deep into a distant jungle. Hidden within its heart, beneath the heavy shadows of ancient trees, he had glimpsed a mysterious cave.

The elders had spoken of it in hushed tones-the Forbidden Cave, said to reveal itself only in the darkest hour of Bistaria's fate.

Without wasting a moment, Teksh raced toward the forest, his hooves striking the ground with fierce determination. The wind howled through the trees as he reached the cave's entrance.

It was shrouded in darkness, invisible to ordinary eyes-but Teksh, born of magic, could see it clearly. Strange markings glowed faintly along the walls-symbols of the old legends, carved to guard secrets of sacred power.

He studied them closely, chanting the ancient words under his breath. Slowly, the carvings pulsed with light and rearranged themselves to form a message that read:

"Two doors guard both truth and end.
One opens to the way forward, one to doom.
Two guardians stand eternal-
one speaks only truth,
the other speaks only lies.
Ask but one question-choose with care-
for only the right words will show the path."

Teksh's heart quickened. As the words faded, the wall before him split apart into two towering stone doors-each flanked by a silent guardian carved from the same rock. One wore a serene smile; the other bore a cold, knowing smirk. Their eyes gleamed like molten gold, watching him with unnerving stillness.

The air thickened with tension. He could ask only one question. One wrong word, and the cave would collapse. Teksh's mind raced. The guardians waited, expressionless. Their presence felt both ancient and endless-like riddles carved before time began.

He drew a deep breath, the wind from the forest swirling around him. "So," he murmured, "only one of you speaks true... and one lies. But which of you guards the way forward?"

He looked from one to the other, thinking, If I ask the right question and only one, both truth and lies will point the same way.

The torches along the cave wall flickered, casting twin shadows across the doors. Teksh closed his eyes for a moment, listening to the symbols around him, and prepared to speak.

(Can you solve the guardian's riddle, before Teksh does?)

Space for you, Thinker *Solution on page 171*

The symbols pulsed once-then fell still, as though holding their breath for the answer. A low hum rippled through the cave, and the stone gate ahead began to shudder, its carvings splitting down the center. A thin line of golden light bled through the crack, widening until the passage beyond glowed like the heart of the earth itself.

Teksh stepped cautiously into the cave. The air inside was cool and heavy, carrying the faint scent of old magic. He glanced back once toward the entrance. "For Tiara,", his voice echoing against the stone.

At the far end stood a mirror-tall, ancient, and alive with a strange light. Stars flickered within its surface, swirling as though an entire universe was trapped inside. As Teksh moved closer, the starlight shifted, twisting and bending until it formed a glowing image-his own reflection, but older, wiser, and wrapped in a faint silver aura. Startled, Teksh asked in his alpaca tongue, "Who are you?"

The reflection smiled softly. "I am you - from a world long forgotten," it said. "I have waited through ages for your arrival, knowing that one day you would free me from this spellbound prison. Before I fade, I must warn you. The shadow you fear-Zarkasur-has risen before. He devours worlds, and your time runs short. Only the Sapphire Cube can stop the coming doom."

The reflection's voice deepened, echoing through the cave like a voice carried by time itself.

"Zarkasur comes from a faraway planet called Sakaria," it whispered. "A world where every creature lived and breathed through magic. Once, Sakaria shone with light and wonder, its skies alive and its rivers full of song. But when its magic began to fade, darkness crept in. The land cracked, the air grew still, and even the stars seemed to dim.

Desperate to save his world, Zarkasur gave away his own power to feed the dying land. For a while, Sakaria lived again-but each time he gave, he grew weaker, emptier. The emptiness began to burn inside him, a hunger no act of kindness could fill.

In time, that hunger twisted him. He began to take what he once gave. To restore his strength, he drew magic from other worlds, turning his mercy into greed. What began as the will to protect became the thirst to possess. From his shadow, he forged dark creatures-loyal, ruthless beings who carried his hunger beyond the stars.

Now, his hunger has no end. He searches for new worlds rich in magic... and Bistaria is his next prey."

Teksh's heart pounded as the reflection continued, its eyes glowing with urgency.

"The blue liquid flowing from Tiara's forehead is no wound-it is her life's magic being stolen. Zarkasur has already begun feeding from her, from your people, from every creature in your land. You have only ten days before Bistaria is drained of all magic and left in eternal stillness."

Teksh stepped closer, trembling. "How can I stop him? How can I save Tiara?"

The reflection's gaze softened. "There is only one way," it said. "You must find the Sapphire Cube-a relic forged at the dawn of time. It alone holds the power to bind Zarkasur to Sakaria for another ten thousand years, trapping him within his own world.

Beyond the horizon of Kharkhania lies your path. Cross the raging sea, reach the Dark Forest of Mangurv, hidden behind the storm's heart. There you will find the first of nine pieces of the cube. Gather them all, bring them back here, only then will the seal hold once more."

"You must go now," the reflection urged, its voice fading like wind through old stone. "Do not lose a single moment. If you fail to gather all nine pieces by midnight of the tenth day, the magic of Bistaria will vanish-forever."

A thin beam of light appeared between them, forming into a glowing silver ring. "Give this to Tiara," the reflection said. "When she wears it, the flow of magic from her body will stop. It will protect her-for now.

Light rippled across the mirror's surface, and the reflection's image wavered. From within the glass, a pulse of silver energy reached out and touched the ring. A faint symbol-a crescent intertwined with a flame-blossomed across its surface, glowing softly before fading into the metal.

"This ring carries a memory of me," the reflection said softly. "When the path grows dark and you no longer know the way, you may call upon me once more. Rub the ring, and my echo will awaken - but only once. After that, the memory will fade, but the ring will remain-a quiet guardian, keeping her magic from ever slipping away again."

Teksh's eyes widened. "So, you'll come back?"
"Only if your hearts remain true," the reflection replied. "Use it not for fear, but for faith."
Go, Teksh. Go before it's too late."

Teksh's heart thundered. Fear and hope raced through him in equal measure. For the first time since Zarkasur's arrival, there was a way-dangerous, uncertain, but real. He dashed out of the cave with blinding speed, his hooves striking sparks from the rocks.

Within moments, he reached Tiara and breathlessly told her everything he had learned. Without hesitation, she slipped the glowing ring onto her finger. At once, the blue liquid on her forehead began to dry and fade. A wave of relief washed over her face.

Wasting no time, they readied their small raft. Bhavam and Rivaaya stood at the riverbank, pride and worry shining in their eyes. "Be brave, my child," her mother says softly. "The river will guide you."

As they pushed off, Teksh-eager and nervous-galloped ahead to help, only to skid straight into a hay cart near the edge of the village. Even in their tears, the villagers burst into laughter, and Tiara smiled through hers. "That's my Teksh," she said softly, her voice full of love and courage, as their journey began.

****

Chapter 4 – The Golden Door (Puzzle II)

They began their journey beyond the horizon of Kharkhania. For the first time, the comforting shores of Bistaria vanished behind them, swallowed by distance and mist. No longer could they see Bhavam, Rivaaya, or the warm glow of their village-only the endless stretch of dark water and the haunting reflection of an ember-red sky. The river's gentle song had turned into the restless roar of the open sea.

Before them stretched an endless sea - dark waters swirling under the red glow of Zarkasur's distant light. His shadow hung over the world like a curse, watching their every move.

As dusk fell, the wind grew colder, fiercer. Tiara held onto the raft's edge, her eyes widening as a vast wall of swirling darkness began to rise ahead of them. A sea storm-massive and alive-was charging toward them with thunderous might. The waves twisted like living beasts, and flashes of lightning painted monstrous shapes in the sky.

Teksh's gaze hardened. He remembered the words of his reflection in the cave: "Go to the Deep Dark Forest of Mangurv, hidden beyond the heart of the storm." He knew what it meant now. They would have to cross this thunderstorm-no matter how wild, no matter how impossible - to reach their next destination.

As the raft neared the heart of the swirling chaos, the sea roared and lightning split the sky open like a burning scar. The winds howled with such force that the air itself seemed alive. And then-just when it felt like the storm would swallow them whole-a massive golden door appeared within the cyclone, hovering in midair.

It sparkled like sunlight trapped inside glass, unmoving even as the furious waves crashed around it. Each flash of lightning revealed strange, swirling symbols etched across its surface-patterns that seemed to dance between light and shadow. Tiara stared in awe. It was beautiful, terrifying, and utterly impossible.

The letters on the door shimmered, rearranging themselves into glowing script. The words pulsed as though alive, their golden edges rippling like waves of light:

"To cross this storm, answer what binds light and shadow as one. Fail, and the sea shall claim your path forever."

The storm roared louder, testing their courage. Tiara reached out toward the golden door, though it hovered far beyond her grasp. As her fingers stretched into the air, a pulse of warmth answered from afar-an unseen thread connecting her to the door's glow.

Blue sparks of light flickered across the carvings. Then, like ripples in water, the symbols began to move, forming glowing lines that beat softly like a heart. The lines intertwined into patterns-then letters-as the first words of the puzzle began to form.

"Within one home live three flames," the door whispered. "Their multiplied strength burns with thirty-six sparks of life. Yet their total sparks, when counted one by one, matched a number well known to the traveler who once sought their glow.

Even knowing that number, he could not tell their sparks apart - until the brightest began her chant beneath the silver moon."

Tiara tilted her head. "Three flames… their multiplied sparks are thirty-six… and one chants under the moon?" Teksh's ears flicked thoughtfully "Their pattern must fit both their strength and their count."

Tiara smiled faintly. "That brightest flame-the one whose chant rises above the rest-must be the key."

Outside, thunder rolled across the sky, shaking the very air. The golden door glimmered faintly, waiting.

The air stilled. The storm seemed to listen.

If they spoke the right answer, the golden door would open.

(Can you figure out the individual sparks of the three flames, before Tiara does?)

Space for you, Thinker *Solution on page 173*

The moment Tiara spoke the answer, the carvings blazed to life, flooding the storm with gold. Symbols rippled across the door, weaving into three perfect spirals of light-two glowing alike, and one shining brighter than the rest.

Thunder rolled through the heavens as if the world itself had heard their answer. The golden door quivered, then swirled into a single beam of radiant light that speared skyward-waiting, daring them to step through.

Side by side, Tiara and Teksh faced the light. The door flared with light, dissolved, and pulled them in.

When the glow faded, Tiara steadied herself, her heart still echoing with the storm's roar.

"Two doors, two riddles," she murmured. "Perhaps the river was testing us."

Teksh's ears flicked. "Testing-for what?"

"For something greater," Tiara said softly, her gaze fixed on the horizon. "I can feel it… our real journey has only begun."

And with that, their true quest began

The Quest of the Sapphire Cube!!!

Chapter 5 – Where Rivers Rise (Puzzle III)

On the other side, they found themselves standing in a forest unlike any they had ever seen-the Forest of Mangurv. A deep, endless darkness cloaked everything; not even a single ray of light pierced through the towering trees. The air felt heavy and filled with a soft, unseen magic. Tiara could see only one thing - the warm golden light of Teksh's eyes shining at her in the darkness.

Then, she remembered her mother Rivaaya's words-the Lumos Chant, taught only to those pure of heart. Taking a deep breath, Tiara hymns the sacred words. Instantly, the crescent on her forehead began to glow, faint at first, then bright and radiant. The darkness retreated, and the entire forest came alive.

Silver leaves glimmered overhead like constellations, and the ground sparkled as if dusted with starlight. As they walked deeper, the air quivered with light, each breath filled with the scent of dew and old secrets. Then, through the glowing mist, they reached a clearing-and there it stood: a waterfall unlike any other.

Instead of tumbling down, the crystal-blue water streamed upward, soaring gracefully into the sky. Droplets twinkled like tiny stars, rising into a whirl of golden mist that disappeared beyond the treetops. The sound it made was strange and beautiful-like a song sung backward through time.

Tiara and Teksh stood silent, their eyes wide with wonder. They knew this was no ordinary place. This was the heart of magic itself-the place where the world's enchantment was born and where their great adventure was about to begin.

When they reached the base of the waterfall, Tiara gasped. Behind the upward surge of glowing water, a single stone pulsed with radiant blue light. It was unmistakable-the first piece of the Sapphire Cube.

Teksh's eyes gleamed. Without hesitation, he leapt into the silver-lit river, cutting through the currents with powerful strokes. But as he neared the waterfall, an invisible force struck him back. Again and again, he tried to break through, yet the rising water refused to let him pass. It was as if the falls themselves guarded the treasure.

Tiara's sharp eyes scanned the rocks nearby, searching for another way. That's when she noticed a bright pink marble half-buried in the sand, glowing faintly with ancient carvings. Kneeling beside it, she brushed away the moss and read the inscription aloud:

"To claim the cube, prove your worth.

Solve this riddle, and the water shall obey."

Tiara paused. Puzzles were her gift-but this time, a wrong answer could bring danger not just to her, but to the entire world. The thought sent a tremor through her heart. Still, she took a deep breath and says to herself, "I have to try."

The marble brightened, projecting an image - a narrow, swaying bridge stretching across an endless chasm. Four tiny glowing figures appeared at its edge, carrying a single flickering torch.

A voice rose from the marble, deep and ancient as the tide:

"Four travelers must cross the Moon Bridge on or before the seventeenth heartbeat of dawn.

At max, two can cross at once. They must move at the pace of the slower one.

A flame must guide their path back and forth-for without its light, the bridge will vanish, and the darkness will consume them."

The glowing figures shimmered, each marked by a different hue.

"The first," said the voice, "moves with the swiftness of one heartbeat.

The second follows close behind, like a shadow, in two heartbeats.

The third walks steady and sure in seven heartbeats.

The fourth, burdened by age and armour, takes ten heartbeats to cross."

Tiara studied the bridge of light where the figures waited. "Only two can walk at once... and they must share the same flame. Each time it returns, more heartbeats pass."

Teksh nodded gravely. "Then every moment matters. The wrong pair could lose them to the dawn."

The pink marble pulsed once, as if listening, then stilled-waiting for their answer.

(Can you figure out how the four travelers can cross the bridge on or before the seventeenth heartbeat of dawn – before Tiara does?)

Space for you, Thinker *Solution on page 175*

As the final heartbeat echoed through the air, the carvings on the pink marble blazed to life. A deep tremor rippled through the ground, and the roaring waterfall before them began to slow. The rushing wall of water thinned, flashed with brilliance - and then parted like a curtain of glass.

Behind it, nestled in the glistening rock, a radiant shard of the Sapphire Cube emerged. It pulsed softly in midair-cold as moonlight, yet burning with a quiet, inner fire. Its glow washed over their faces in hues of sapphire and gold, as if it held both ice and flame within a single breath of magic.

Tiara stepped forward, her pulse racing, and reached out. The first piece of the Sapphire Cube was finally hers.

She held it gently, feeling its low vibration against her palm before slipping it safely into her pocket. When she looked at Teksh, a quiet determination settled over her. One day had already passed, and every heartbeat now carried the weight, and hope, of everyone waiting back home in Bistaria.

The waterfall roared back to life, surging upward once more. In moments, the path behind them vanished beneath the churning water. Tiara and Teksh stood stranded on the far side, the spray cold against their faces.

They tried shouting, searching, even testing the edges of the glowing stream-but every route was sealed by the restless water. Panic flickered in Tiara's chest. The air felt heavy, closing in. The roar of the falls drowned every thought, every hope.

Her gaze fell to the silver ring on her finger - the one Teksh had given her in Bistaria. Its glow, once faint and fading, now throbbed softly in time with the Cube's light. For a moment, she just stared at it, unsure if it was truly answering or if it was her own fear willing it to shine.

She hesitated, then utters, "You said we could call him… maybe he can still hear us."

She rubbed the ring gently beneath the soft glow of the waterfall's reflection. The air rippled softly - and then, through the glistening veil of water, a familiar image began to take shape. It was Teksh's reflection, glowing with soft silver light-the same holographic spirit he had encountered in the cave.

The reflection spoke in a calm yet urgent voice.

"You have found the first shard of the Sapphire Cube," the reflection said, its voice steady and low, like an echo carried through time. "But this is only the beginning. There are nine shards in all, scattered across the realms of this world. You now hold one. Remaining shards still await your courage."

Tiara's breath caught. "Eight more to go", she exclaimed, determination sparking in her eyes.

The image nodded. "Each shard is guarded by a power - one that cannot be defeated by strength alone. Only the union of wit and love can reveal the path to each. Remember that, Tiara. For as your mind solves the riddles of life, your heart must stay pure. That is the only way to restore the Sapphire Cube's light."

The air trembled softly, and the reflection's gaze deepened, glowing with silver fire. "When you touched the shard, Zarkasur felt it. He knows now that the Cube has awakened. He feeds on fear, and courage burns him. From this moment onward, every step you take will be watched."

The figure's eyes glowed brighter. "Your next path lies in the Land of Fire. Go to the end of this cave, and you will find a narrow trail that leads there. But remember-the fire tests not your strength, but your heart."

Before Tiara could speak, the image flickered and vanished into thin air, leaving only the echo of magic in the air. She turned to Teksh, who nodded silently. They both understood-the journey ahead would test more than their courage.

That night, they decided to rest within the cave, its glowing walls flickering gently like fireflies. A quiet smile touched their faces as they watched the gentle light dance across the stone. The first piece of the cube was more than just a fragment of stone-it was hope, a spark strong enough to challenge the darkness spreading from Sakaria.

Meanwhile, in distant Bistaria, Zarkasur's blood-red eyes snapped open again. His massive form stirred, his dark aura pulsing with rage. He had felt it-the disturbance in magic. Someone was seeking the Sapphire Cube.

"Who dares..." his voice rumbled, shaking the sky of Bistaria.

At once, he sent a piercing mind-signal across the void to his most trusted warrior-Biraksha, commander of the Dark Forces. Cunning and merciless, Biraksha had helped him conquer countless worlds. As the signal reached him, Biraksha's eyes ignited with red flame.

Without a word, Biraksha rose from the shadows, his black armour gleaming like molten stone beneath the storm-lit skies of Sakaria. The air around him cracked with dark energy as he surged upward, carried not by wings but by sheer force of will. Lightning bent to his command as he tore through the storm clouds, crossing realms in a blur of darkness.

His mission was clear - find the ones seeking the Cube, and end their journey before it even begins.

****

Chapter 6 – The Trial of the Flames (Puzzle IV)

Day 2 dawned dim and restless as Tiara and Teksh made their way through the winding tunnels of the cave, following the trail of magic that led toward the Land of Fire. The air grew warmer with every step, and soon, the rough stone walls gave way to an opening-a narrow, glowing path stretching across a bottomless void.

Far ahead, they could see it: an island wreathed in flame, its surface flickering like molten gold. Teksh leapt first onto the path but immediately skidded forward, his hooves scraping the edge. Tiara gasped and grabbed his fur just in time, pulling him back to safety.

"You and your crashes!" she giggles, breathless, half-scolding and half-laughing.

The path ahead was narrower than they imagined, a ribbon of light suspended over an endless void. On either side, darkness stretched infinitely-cold, silent, and unforgiving. The narrow trail pulsed beneath their feet, carrying them forward as if guiding their every step. Ahead, the air shimmered in hues of crimson and gold-the first glimpse of the Land of Fire.

The closer they moved, the hotter the air became. The flames rose and fell in rhythmic waves, yet none touched them; the blessings of Bistaria shielded their bodies in a soft halo of light. Beneath their feet, the glowing path began to fade into scorched ground, and they realized they had crossed the threshold.

Flames coiled and hissed around them like serpents, the heat pressing close but never daring to harm. In the island's heart lay a vast pit of molten rock-alive, restless, breathing light into the dark sky. On a single stone ledge in the middle, a shard of the Sapphire Cube floated in a halo of ruby glow, turning slowly as if waiting for them.

Tiara's eyes widened. "There it is," she says excitedly.

But before they could move closer, the air in front of them twisted wildly. From the molten pit rose a towering sentinel made of smoke and fire-its form half-human, half-inferno. Its body rippled like molten glass, with veins of fire running beneath the surface. Where its eyes should have been, empty hollows glowed faintly inside a fiery skull, giving it a look both haunting and powerful.

Tiara froze, gripping Teksh's fur tightly. "What... what is that?" she whispered.

Teksh lowered his stance, ready to leap if needed. "Whatever it is," he muttered, "it's guarding the cube."

The sentinel's voice rumbled like an earthquake. "Few dare set foot on the Land of Fire," it said, each word echoing through the heat. "And fewer still walk away."

Tiara took a cautious step forward. "We're not here to steal-we're here to save our world."

For a long moment, the sentinel was silent. Then the flames within its chest flared brighter, and its voice rumbled through the air, both warning and test. The ground beneath them shook as it declared: "To reach the shard, you must pass the Trial of the Flames."

Tiara clenched her fists but kept her voice steady. "Then tell us the trial. We're not afraid of your fire."

The sentinel leaned forward, its molten form crackling. "Bravery is easy to claim, child," it said. "Wisdom decides if it burns or endures."

The air thickened with heat as its voice deepened again, echoing through the fiery island:

"A thousand goblets stand before you.

One holds a silent curse; the rest hold harmless elixirs. You may send chosen number of souls to taste, but the curse reveals itself only after one full turn of the sun.

Once tasted, no soul may drink again from the same goblet." The air grew still. Even the lava seemed to pause its bubbling.

The sentinel's voice softened into an almost human: "Tell me, seeker of balance - what is the least number of souls you must send to discover the single cursed goblet? Know this - the number is fewer than thirteen."

Tiara stared into the molten pit, her brow furrowed. "A thousand goblets… and the curse shows itself only after a day… no one can drink twice from the same goblet."

Teksh's voice rumbled quietly beside her. "It's fewer than thirteen-that means there's a smart way to test them, not just luck."

Tiara nodded. "If each soul drinks from a different mix of goblets, their fates - their changes of light - whose glow endures and whose dims - will form a message. The pattern itself will point to the cursed goblet."

She paused, thinking aloud. "So, each soul's choice becomes a line of light or shadow-together, they can mark one goblet from a thousand."

The carvings on the cave wall began to pulse with faint golden light, as if waiting for her to find the number.

(Can you find the number of fewest souls Tiara needs to send to discover which goblet is cursed, knowing it is fewer than thirteen?)

Space for you, Thinker

Solution on page 177

As the last symbol flared bright, the answer echoed like a heartbeat. The golden carvings dimmed-acknowledging her triumph-and the ghost stirred. It was not easy, but with Tiara's sharp mind, no riddle was beyond her reach.

The ghost's hollow eyes flickered-half respect, half warning. Then, with a roar that shook the island, he lifted his blazing axe. Its molten edge sliced the air, sending a shockwave across the pit.

The ground shuddered. Cracks spread like lightning as the narrow path began to crumble, piece by piece, sinking into the lava below. The ghost's echoing voice thundered through the flames, "Cross quickly while the path still breathes! Once you claim the second piece, hold tight to the cliff-or be lost forever!"

Without hesitation, Tiara and Teksh charged across the trembling path. Lava sprayed on both sides like sparks from an angry forge. Tiara leapt and reached the centre cliff first-but Teksh was still five steps behind when the final segment began to break apart.

"Teksh!" Tiara shouted.

With one mighty push of his legs, Teksh jumped through the fiery mist and landed squarely in Tiara's arms. For a heartbeat, they both sat frozen-then burst into laughter, their fear melting away. After so much danger, it felt good to laugh again.

Before them hovered the second shard of the Sapphire Cube, spinning gently above the molten pit. Tiara reached out, her hand trembling slightly, and as her fingers brushed its surface, the shard glowed and connected instantly with the first piece tucked safely in her pocket. The cube pulsing softly like a living heart.

Remembering the ghost's warning, Tiara gripped the edge of the cliff tightly, Teksh bracing beside her. The lava beneath began to swirl violently, rising higher and higher like a living tide. Then, to their astonishment, the cliff itself started to move-lifting, stretching, climbing upward through the clouds of smoke and fire.

Higher and higher it rose, bursting through the black storm clouds until the world below vanished into swirling red mist. For the first time in what felt like forever, sunlight touched their faces. The sky around them glowed gold and white, clear and pure.

Tiara and Teksh stood together on the floating cliff, eyes wide with wonder. After all the darkness, they were finally surrounded by light again-but neither knew what awaited them above.

****

Chapter 7 – The Aether Egg (Puzzle V)

Suddenly, a shadow swept across the molten horizon. A giant eagle descended from the blazing sky, its wings spanning wider than a house, casting a cool twilight over the fiery land below.

With a single, powerful beat of its wings, it lifted Tiara and Teksh from the rising heat, carrying them high into the clouds. The wind roared around them, but the eagle's grip was steady and strong, her feathers glowing faintly with traces of ancient magic.

She carried them away from the flames to the tallest tree they could see - a huge trunk that seemed to touch the sky. At the very top was her enormous nest, made of golden reeds and soft, shining feathers. Gently, the eagle set Tiara and Teksh down inside it, then spread her great wings and flew off into the glowing sky.

The air still smelled of salt and smoke, and in the middle of the nest lay an extraordinary, round egg that glowed faintly among bits of fish bones and cooled ash.

As the red sun sank below the horizon, turning the world golden and dim, Tiara and Teksh shared a quiet look. The storm was over. They were tired, but for the first time in a long while, they felt safe - even if only for a while. They rested in the eagle's nest that night, as the rumble of the molten island slowly faded into the calm rhythm of sleep.

When dawn came, the first rays of sunlight passed through the clouds, painting the nest in soft shades of gold and pink. Tiara woke, her eyes catching a faint glow at the centre of the nest. She sat up slowly, her breath catching in wonder.

The egg was unlike anything she had ever seen. Its shell was smooth and cool, shaped not by nature but by something greater. Thin lines of shifting light ran beneath its surface, pulsing softly like living magic. It didn't seem alive - yet it beat faintly, as if something inside was waiting to awaken... a heartbeat made of light and silence.

Moments later, the eagle returned, wings glinting in the morning light. She landed beside the nest and settled gently over the egg, her sharp golden eyes studying Tiara and Teksh.

To their surprise, the eagle spoke in their language- her voice deep, roughened by time, yet clear. Perhaps she had learned it over the long, lonely years of waiting for someone to come.

"Why did you bring us here?" Teksh asked respectfully. "And why does this egg feel... different?"

The eagle bowed her great head, her voice deep and filled with quiet sorrow.

"I came to help you," she said. "Long ago, I lived on Adipur - a world of endless skies and singing winds. The air there was bright and alive, and our wings painted the heavens with colours of dawn. It was a paradise of birds and light, where every breeze carried a song."

Her eyes darkened, the weight of memory heavy in her gaze. "But then Zarkasur came. He drained the magic from our lands and swallowed the wind's voice. One by one, my kin fell silent - their songs fading into dust. The skies grew empty, and the sun no longer rose with joy. Now, I am the last of my kind."

For a moment, she lifted her wings slightly, their edges catching the soft glow of the dying day. "I have flown across a thousand storms, searching for a spark of the old magic. And when I felt the Cube awaken, I knew that hope still lived."

Her gaze turned to Tiara, warm and resolute. "You carry that hope now, child. Let it lift you higher than my wings ever could."

She paused, her eyes drifting toward the glowing egg nestled at the heart of the nest. "Before our world fell, I found one piece of the Sapphire Cube. But when I touched it, it changed-becoming this Aether egg. Since then, it has slept beneath my wings, its light fading with each passing year." Her voice trembled softly. "Behind it lies a carving - a riddle I could never solve. So, I have guarded it all this time, waiting for someone worthy… someone brave enough to claim it."

Teksh turned to Tiara, his voice low with awe. "It's one of the pieces," he said. Together, they approached the egg.

As Tiara brushed away the ash and feathers, faint glowing lines appeared across its smooth surface, forming ancient symbols. Slowly, the carvings brightened, revealing words etched in living light.

Then, with a soft pulse, the egg began to vibrate softly. Its glow stretched upward, forming a thin golden beam that pierced the smoky sky above.

High in the heavens, one star flickered to life - brighter than all the rest - as if awakened by the egg's call. Its silver light reflected in Tiara's eyes, and from it came a voice, soft and distant, fading like a bell:

"Two numbers were chosen. Their multiplied strength was eight… or perhaps it was sixteen."

Tiara looked up, puzzled. "Who said that?" she asked. "No one I know," Teksh replied. "But it's a starting thread - two numbers, with one of two possible strengths."

As the star's light trembled, two faint silhouettes appeared over the Aether Egg - figures made of smoke and thought. They faced each other and began to speak, their voices low and deliberate, as if sharing a secret, they barely understood.

The first silhouette spoke, its voice rough like shifting stone.

"I don't know your number."

The second answered softly.

"I don't know your number."

The first repeated, slower this time.

"I don't know your number."

And again, the second replied,

"I don't know your number."

Then, after a long pause - the first silhouette spoke once more, its tone now sure.

"Now I know your number."

The shapes dissolved, and the star overhead dimmed, returning to its place among the heavens.

But the riddle lingered - revolving faintly around the Aether Egg, a puzzle woven from logic and light.

From the fragments of that brief, stubborn conversation, what number had the second silhouette been holding all along?

Tiara stared at the fading glow, she says softly. "Five exchanges… and one truth revealed."

(Can you figure out the number which second silhouette was holding, before Tiara does?)

Space for you, Thinker *Solution on page 179*

For a heartbeat, nothing happened. Then the air quivered-gentle at first, then alive with golden ripples, as if the egg had taken its first breath. With a thunderous crack, the marble egg split open, releasing a blinding beam of golden light that spiraled into the heavens.

From its core, the glowing shard of the Sapphire Cube emerged, soaring gracefully before joining the other pieces in Tiara's pocket. The eagle let out a triumphant cry, her feathers glinting like molten gold as she spread her vast wings.

The scorched winds bowed beneath her wings as she rose, lifting Tiara and Teksh high above the blazing land. The air burst with heat and magic, and for a fleeting moment, it felt as if they were flying straight into the heart of a sunrise, chasing destiny itself.

The eagle's sharp eyes gleamed with ancient knowing. "Beyond this horizon lies your next trial," she said softly, her voice carried by the wind. "The clue rests not upon the land, but deep within the ocean's heart-hidden beneath the North Star's eternal gaze."

As she spoke, waves below sparkled with ghostly blue light, as if acknowledging the prophecy.

With a mighty beat of her wings, the eagle lifted Tiara and Teksh into the sky. The air rushed past them as they soared higher and higher, leaving the burning island behind and gliding toward the vast, waiting sea.

Far ahead, the sea turned dark and endless. Tiara felt a chill-not from the cold wind, but from knowing something great and unknown awaited them. Teksh stood firm beside her, and together they looked toward the distant glowing star, where their next journey was waiting.

Suddenly, the eagle sensed danger.

The clouds split apart with a thunderous rumble, and from the swirling mist emerged a towering figure-majestic yet frightening.

His armour shimmered like molten silver, carved with glowing runes that flickered in the lightning's glare. A crimson cape curled behind him, torn at the edges yet defiant, like a banner that had witnessed countless victories.

His eyes burned a deep amber-steady, fearless, and proud-not cruel, but carrying the cold confidence of a warrior who had never known defeat.

Across his back rested a massive blade that thrummed softly, as though it carried the echoes of conquered worlds.

This was no ordinary foe-this was Biraksha, the champion of darkness, born to serve his master's will.

He had come for Tiara-to end her quest before she could save Bistaria. The eagle halted midair, wings stretched against the howling wind. For a moment, none of them moved. The air crackled with tension as their eyes locked.

Then Biraksha's voice cut through the storm, deep and commanding. "You can't go any further. I am here to stop you from collecting the remaining pieces of the cube."

Tiara met his gaze. She had never seen such darkness in anyone's eyes-it wasn't madness, but belief. And that confused her deeply. How could anyone choose evil over kindness?

Her voice trembled at first but soon steadied with resolve. "We won't stop until Zarkasur is sent back to his world. If you value your life, return to yours."

Biraksha let out a low, mocking laugh. "Return? To the world Zarkasur has rebuilt with his power? You speak as if you understand strength." His eyes narrowed. "You're just a frightened child playing hero."

Tiara's grip tightened on the eagle's feathers. "I may be a child," she said firmly, "but I still know right and wrong. That's something your world seems to have forgotten."

Biraksha's smile faded. The air around him throbbed with dark energy as he rose from his black cloud, his blade glowing faintly red. "Enough talk. I'll carve that courage out of you myself."

He thrust his arm forward, and the air cracked. With a roar that shook the skies, Biraksha leapt high, his blade slicing through the air like lightning.

The eagle twisted sharply, and Tiara gripped its feathers tightly, her heart pounding. Teksh almost slipped but pressed his hooves into the straps and held on.

Biraksha attacked again, but the eagle beat her powerful wings, blasting him backward with a rush of wind.

"He's strong, but clumsy when he attacks!" Tiara shouted, watching his rhythm closely.

Biraksha roared, spinning through the air. His blade scraped across the eagle's wing, scattering silver feathers into the storm. The mighty bird cried out, dipping dangerously as pain shot through her wing. Tiara gasped, fear tightening her chest - but she couldn't give up now.

"Teksh-distract him!" she yelled.

Teksh ran along the eagle's back and jumped. He slammed into Biraksha mid-swing, sending both spinning through the dark clouds. The eagle fought to stay aloft, her wounded wing trembling with every beat.

As Tiara steadied herself, her hand brushed against the saddlebag-and she felt something warm inside. She pulled out a small glass jar that glowed faintly blue. Rivaaya had given it to her long ago, saying it was made to hold lost or wandering magic until its purpose was found. Tiara had never understood it-until now.

Biraksha steadied himself again, fury blazing in his eyes. Lightning danced across his armour as he charged. Tiara gripped the straps tighter, her hair whipping wildly in the wind. "Now!" she shouted.

Teksh kicked off, throwing his weight against the rope as Tiara cast it forward. The loop caught perfectly. With the eagle's sharp twist, Biraksha lost balance and fell straight into the glowing jar that had risen open in front of him.

"For Kharkhania," Tiara shouts, her voice trembling yet strong. The jar sealed itself with a flash of blue fire as Biraksha's roar faded into the storm.

She fastened the glowing jar to her keeper's belt. The battle had taken its toll. As sky painted the horizon in shades of gold, the eagle's wingbeats slowed, weary but steady. Above them, the North Star burned bright and unwavering-a silent reminder of where they needed to go.

The eagle spread her mighty wings once more, summoning every ounce of remaining strength. With a final surge of speed, she soared across the dark waters, cutting through the wind like a comet. In what felt like moments, they reached the far edge of the ocean.

But the effort had drained her completely. The wound from Biraksha's blade burned along her wing, its silver feathers now streaked with ash and blood. Her wings trembled as she landed on the jagged rocks, her breathing shallow, her magic fading. Yet her eyes still gleamed with pride - a final spark of courage before the light dimmed.

Tiara slid from her back, pressing her face into the eagle's warm feathers, unwilling to let go. Teksh moved close, silent and still, as if understanding the gravity of the moment.

The eagle lifted her head weakly and released one final cry-half song, half farewell. Her body began to sparkle, dissolving into countless silver sparks that drifted upward, merging with the sky.

Tiara watched, her chest heavy with grief, yet beneath the sorrow burned a fierce determination. Their friend's sacrifice would not be in vain.

As night fell, Tiara and Teksh rested by the ocean's edge, preparing for the next day's journey. The waves dashes softly against the rocks, but Tiara could not sleep. She sat curled by the shore, gazing at the spot where the eagle's light had disappeared.

“I used to think love was enough to keep everyone safe,” she mumbles. “But now I know love can’t stop goodbye - it just stays behind when they’re gone”.

Teksh curled beside her, unusually quiet. His soft breath was steady, grounding her. Tiara reached for the magical jar at her belt-the one holding Biraksha-and clenched it tightly. The loss of her friend had carved something new inside her: not just sorrow, but determination.

“If she gave her last flight for us, then I cannot fail,” Tiara thought. She wiped her tears, lifted her chin toward the North Star, and felt her courage harden like steel. Tomorrow, the journey would continue.

****

Chapter 8 - Whispers of the Drowned (Puzzle VI)

The next morning - Day 4 - Tiara sat by the shore, lost in thought. Somewhere in the vast depths of the ocean lay the next piece of the Sapphire Cube. But how could she reach it? No human could dive that far and live.

Her eyes drifted toward the horizon where the sky met the sea. She thought of Bistaria - of her parents, the villagers, and the fading glow of Kharkhania. Every moment they lost, Zarkasur grew stronger. The cube was their only hope, and failure was not an option.

Tiara clenched her fists, feeling the weight of her world on her small shoulders. She had to find a way, no matter how impossible it seemed.

Teksh, sensing her worry, pawed the sand with quiet confidence. He was no ordinary creature-he carried the spirit of Kharkhania within him, shaped by its waves and blessed by its magic. Without a moment's hesitation, he leapt into the ocean, cutting through the surface like a golden streak of light.

Down he went, deeper and deeper, the water growing darker, colder. Then-crash! Even underwater, Teksh couldn't quite master his stops. He slammed into a coral wall, sending a swirl of glittering bubbles dancing around him. Tiara, watching from above, let out a nervous laugh-her fear easing for just a moment.

But Teksh's laughter didn't follow. His eyes had widened in alarm. Before him loomed, a massive chest guarded by a monstrous, sharklike creature. Its scales shined like forged steel and its fins sliced the water with lethal precision.

Without hesitation, Teksh charged. The sea exploded into motion-bubbles rising, tails whipping, the glint of magic flashing through the depths. Waves churned as the two forces battled beneath the surface. At last, Teksh overpowered the beast, grabbed the enormous chest, and dragged it toward the surface.

He broke through the waves, gasping for breath but triumphant. Tiara's eyes filled with hope-surely, this was the fourth piece of the Sapphire Cube. Teksh struck the chest open with a sharp kick.

Silence. Only seawater and emptiness stared back.

Perplexed but determined, Teksh dove once more, following the same glowing reefs. To his shock, the same chest waited at the bottom-as if time itself had reset. Its golden edges shined faintly in the dim light, untouched by their earlier struggle. He swam closer, wary, the memory of the last fight flickering in his mind.

Again-the chest, the battle, the victory. And again... nothing.

He stared at the empty box, heart pounding. The sea around him felt colder now, heavier, as though it were hiding something more than water.

This time, when he surfaced, even the waves seemed uneasy. Tiara felt a chill creep up her spine. Something was wrong.

Determined, Teksh plunged a third time, this time studying carefully. That's when the shark struck from behind. His cry rippled through the ocean, reaching Tiara's heart like lightning.

Without a thought, she dove in after him. The water pressed cold and heavy against her, but her focus was unshaken. A moment later, she gasped - yet no bubbles escaped her lips. She could breathe. The water felt alive around her, glittering softly as if Kharkhania itself welcomed her beneath its surface.

For a heartbeat, wonder filled her-but it vanished the instant she saw Teksh drifting, still and silent. The gift that amazed her now became her strength. She kicked hard through the current, every beat of her heart echoing with urgency.

Near the chest, she saw Teksh floating motionless- and a flickering light beneath the chest's base.

"It's an illusion," she realized. "A trap to guard the real treasure."

The shark circled, swift and merciless, eyes burning red. But Tiara was ready. The water rippled around her as she twisted aside, feeling the rush of its massive body pass inches away. It came again, faster this time, teeth snapping through trails of bubbles. Tiara darted behind a wall of coral, her heart pounding. She could feel the creature's rage vibrating through the water.

Then it lunged-crashing into the reef with a dull thud that shook the sea floor. Broken coral scattered like sparks in the dark water. Tiara seized the moment-grabbing a sharp fragment and striking at the soft ridge near its gills. The shark thrashed wildly, tail lashing currents into violent spirals. Tiara pushed off a rock, spun around its body, and kicked hard toward its face, her movements guided by instinct and the magic coursing through her veins.

The shark roared in anger, but it was slowing down. Then Tiara spotted a shard of coral glinting in the sunlight near the sand. Thinking fast, she grabbed it and angled it toward the beast. The sudden flash of light struck its eyes, making it thrash and turn away in confusion. Tiara used that moment to surge forward and strike with all her strength. The water trembled around them, and then the great creature went still-weak, wounded, and gasping for breath.

As Tiara watched the giant shape drift in the water, her heart sank. Its red eyes dimmed, no longer wild but full of pain. She realized it had only been guarding something, not attacking for hunger or hate. The coral dust floated between them like tiny stars, and she remembered her mother's words: "True strength lies not in victory, but in mercy."

Tiara swam closer, placing her hand gently on the creature's rough skin. A soft blue light spread from her palm, wrapping around the shark's body. The wound on its side began to fade, and its breathing steadied. The fierce beast relaxed, its eyes turning calm and clear.

Then, before her eyes, its form began to change-the scales glowing brighter, the fins turning to light. The shark's heavy frame melted into the graceful shape of an angel, cloaked in silver water and gentle light. Its voice echoed softly, carrying both sorrow and peace.

"You have freed me from the curse of the Wizard of Zarkasur," it said, bowing its head slightly. "He bound me here to guard what he feared most-the power that could end his own darkness."

Tiara stared, her eyes wide, her heart still racing. She had never seen such light, nor felt such peace.

The angel smiled gently. "You, child of the river, have shown mercy where others would have chosen might. Never forget this-love can reach where strength cannot, and heal what even magic cannot touch."

A warmth spread through Tiara's chest, and her eyes filled with tears that floated like tiny pearls in the water. She nodded silently, unable to speak, her heart full of gratitude and wonder. In that quiet moment, she finally understood what it meant to carry the magic of Kharkhania-not as power, but as kindness.

The angel's light began to fade, its form dissolving into a swirl of luminous mist. Calm returned to the waters, and a faint glow lingered beneath the chest as its voice echoed one last time-soft and distant, like a song carried by the sea.

"Beneath this chest lies a riddle-solve it, and the next piece of the Sapphire Cube will be yours. But remember, Tiara, this test holds more than treasure. The moment you unlock its secret; your friend will awaken. His life and your destiny now flow as one."

Tiara's heart tightened. She looked down at Teksh, still motionless in the water, and then at the luminous script forming below the chest. The angel's final words faded into the ocean's hum as its light scattered into a thousand glowing fragments. Now, it was up to Tiara-to save her friend, and to prove her intellect once again.

She swam closer to the chest and pushed it aside to see what lay beneath. As her hand passed over the surface, new symbols flared to life-spiraling outward in rings of gold. The glow deepened, and the water around her began to tremble.

The light bent and twisted until shapes started forming within it. Then, from the shifting shadows, five spectral figures emerged-ancient mariners, their eyes glowing faintly with the gold of long-buried greed. Broken shells and barnacles covered their armour, and strips of seaweed drifted around them like torn flags.

At their centre stood a tall figure wearing a cracked crown of coral-the leader of the drowned. His voice was rough as stone and echoing as the deep.

"We were five when the ocean took us. Five who once shared one chest of hundred gold coins. But when greed weighed heavier than honour, we bound our souls to a single law."

He raised his trident, and the other four spirits turned toward him in silence.

"One shall divide the treasure. The rest shall judge.

If half or more consent, the sea will let him live. If not-he shall sink again into silence, and another will take his place."

The golden light from the chest flared, scattering over the water in a hundred coins.

A current rose from the depths, speaking the terms in a voice that was neither male nor female, but ancient and vast: "Each soul is selfish, each clever, each cold.

They value life first, gold second, and vengeance third. The leader seeks to keep as much as he dares, yet live to tell the tale.

Tell me, seeker of wisdom - what is the greatest share the leader can claim without being cast into the abyss?"

The five Specters began to argue; their words lost beneath the current. Gold glimmered between their hands, vanishing and reappearing, never staying still.

Tiara pressed her palms together. "Five mariners, a hundred coins, and no mercy among them," she murmured. "He needs three votes to survive-his own and two others. If he gives too little, they'll turn against him. If he gives too much, he loses what he came for. What could be the greatest share the leader can keep?"

Her voice softened as she looked at Teksh's still form beside her. "Balance again… even in greed."

(Can you tell how many gold coins the leader will keep for himself before Tiara does?)

Space for you, Thinker *Solution on page 183*

The ocean moved softly, as if her words had awakened something ancient below. The lid trembled and slowly opened with a deep, echoing sound-a sound that seemed to travel through the water, the sand, and even Tiara's heartbeat. Inside was a spinning pool of light, swirling like captured starlight.

She leaned closer. The light rippled outward, revealing the deep sea below-its waves glimmering like liquid glass, stretching into endless blue. At the centre, glowing faintly in the stillness, floated the fourth piece of the Sapphire Cube. It looked weightless, almost shy, as if it had been waiting for her all along.

Tiara reached out slowly. Her fingertips brushed the shard, and warmth flooded through her veins-a warmth that wasn't fire, but memory. She felt hints of laughter, songs of the river, and the faint hum of every creature she had met. The shard pulsed brighter, as though recognizing her touch. Then, with a sudden burst of light, it slipped from her grasp and shot upward, joining the other fragments.

The pieces hovered together, spinning in perfect rhythm, then locked into place, forming one luminous face of the cube. Upon it appeared a radiant pink-and-red heart-softly beating, like something alive. Its light spilled over the water, painting Tiara and Teksh in shades of warmth and rose gold.

The heart drifted forward and touched Teksh's forehead. A soft glow spread through him, pulsing in time with the heart. His body moved, his breathing deepened, and then-his eyes fluttered open, bright and full of life once more.

For a moment, neither moved. Then Teksh leapt with a burst of joy, sending a thousand water droplets flying around them like tiny stars. Tiara laughed through her tears, her voice trembling with relief and love. Teksh pressed his damp nose to her cheek, his warmth mingling with the sea breeze, and for the first time in many days, the world felt whole again.

****

Chapter 9 - The Dwarfs of Kadmirah (Puzzle VII)

When she looked back into the chest, Tiara gasped. Below her was a world she could hardly believe-an ocean hanging upside down in the sky, its waves shining like stars. Floating mountains drifted gently through the air, and trees grew sideways along unseen paths. Rivers of light flowed between them, glowing in every color. Crystals hung above, scattering tiny rainbows all around. Bright fish moved through the air as if swimming, and huge flowers floated open, their glowing petals singing faintly like living stars.

The entire realm seemed to breathe - alive, endless, and filled with the pulse of magic itself.

They understood - it was their next destination. Without hesitation, Tiara and Teksh leapt into the chest. It closed behind them with a flash, sinking peacefully back into place.

Tiara and Teksh drifted slowly into the new world, light as feathers. There was no gravity here - only gentle movement, guided by their thoughts. The air around them glowed with soft colours that kept changing-pink, green, blue, and gold - and every breath felt warm and bright, like breathing light itself.

For a moment, neither of them spoke. It was too beautiful to disturb.

It took time to get used to this strange place. Each step felt slow and dreamlike, as if the world itself was studying them. Tiny glowing orbs floated past, leaving trails of silver light in the air. A cluster of bright fish swam above them, moving through the sky like ripples in water. Tiara reached out her hand, and one of them brushed her fingers before darting away.

They began searching for the next piece of the Sapphire Cube. After a while, Tiara noticed something strange. All the living things around them-the floating petals, the shining vines, even the small glowing creatures-seemed to bend or turn in one direction. It was as if the whole world was drawn toward a single point.

Following their gaze, Tiara saw it-a tree taller than any mountain she had ever known. It rose endlessly into the glowing sky, its trunk twisting gently like a spiral of life. Its bark changed colours with every heartbeat-green, gold, violet-and the air near it smelled of sweet mist and soft rain. The closer they moved, the quieter everything became, as though even the air was holding its breath.

At the centre of the great tree, inside a hollow glowing with pale blue light, floated the fifth piece of the Sapphire Cube. Tiara's heart beat faster. "It's here," she exclaimed. She placed her hand on the trunk and began to climb carefully, her feet pressing against the smooth, warm bark. Teksh followed below, watching her every step.

When Tiara reached the hollow, she stretched out her hand. The piece was close-so close she could almost feel its pulse. But the moment her fingers neared the shard, the world around them changed.

The light faded. The air filled with a sudden, terrible sound-like thousands of cries echoing through the sky. The glowing flowers closed and turned dark. The gentle colours of the world bled into blackness. The great tree trembled, its shining bark turning grey, then jet black. The sweet scent of rain vanished, replaced by cold air and silence.

Tiara froze, her hand trembling in midair. "What's happening?" she whispered. Teksh growled softly, standing guard beside the roots, his eyes glowing faintly in the darkness.

The silence that followed was heavy and strange. The air that once felt warm now grew cold, almost sharp. The glowing rivers that had flowed between the floating islands began to fade, turning pale like dying embers. Tiara's reflection on the bark flickered, and for a moment, she saw not herself-but a shadow of the world's fear.

She pulled her hand back, breathing hard. "This piece… it's the life source," she says. "If I take it, this world dies." The thought struck her like a weight pressing against her chest. She looked around-the glowing creatures that once danced in the air now hid among the branches, their lights dim. The great tree's heart seemed to beat slower.

Teksh stepped closer and nuzzled her arm, as if reminding her she wasn't alone. His soft, steady breath calmed her trembling hands. For a moment, he looked down at the silver ring glowing faintly on Tiara's finger-the same ring that had stopped her magic from fading away.

He closed his eyes and tried to call upon Teksh's reflection again, hoping the light would return. But this time, nothing happened. The ring stayed cold and dull, its magic spent. Teksh's ears drooped, and a quiet sadness passed between them.

Tiara lowered her hand, feeling the weight of silence around them. "Maybe this is the end," she wondered, her voice barely a breath. For a moment, they both stood still, surrounded by the quiet, empty air.

Then Teksh looked up at the towering tree, its fading colours still pulsing faintly like a dying heartbeat. Tiara followed his gaze. With the last spark of hope inside her, she took a deep breath and pressed her palms together.

"Great Tree," she murmured softly, "please show me another way."

The tree listened, the ground beneath her feet began to thrum gently, like the echo of a heartbeat. A faint breeze moved through the darkness, carrying a scent of rain and earth.

A soft resonance rose from deep within the tree-a voice that wasn't a voice, more like a song made of wind and memory. The branches swayed slowly, and the leaves began to glow again, faint at first, then brighter.

Tiara looked up as the air filled with movement. Thousands of leaves loosened and began to fall, drifting downward in soft spirals of light. They twirled gently around her and Teksh, glowing gold and green, lighting up the dark world once more.

Each leaf carried a faint marking-tiny shapes, symbols, and lines that glowed softly like living ink. They floated around Tiara and Teksh, swirling gently in the air. Slowly, the leaves formed a bright circle around Tiara's head before drifting down in front of her.

The symbols began to shine brighter, moving and joining together as if they were alive. Tiara watched in awe as the markings twisted into patterns and then into letters she could read.

The tree had answered. Its voice was not in sound, but in light.

As the last of the leaves fell, they glowed with a faint golden light, weaving themselves into shining words that hung in the air before her –

The Riddle of the Hundred Orbs.

"Beneath my roots lie a hundred hollows," the letters shimmered, "and in each rests an orb of dawn, glowing softly in the dark.

Once each century, the Dwarves of Kadmirah gather in silence at the foot of my trunk to perform the Ritual of Turning - a rite as old as the mountain winds.

One hundred dwarves stand before the hollows; each marked with a number from one to a hundred.

The First Dwarf, bearer of the hammer of dawn, begins the rite. He walks to every hollow, touching each orb once, and with every touch the orb's state change - a bright orb falls to rest, and one at rest awakens.

The Second Dwarf follows, visiting every second hollow - two, four, six, and so on - each time turning light to rest, or rest to light.

The Third Dwarf follows the same path for every third hollow.

The Fourth touches every fourth, and so they continue, one by one, until the Hundredth Dwarf touches only the final orb beneath the farthest root.

When the last step fades into silence, the forest holds its breath once more.

If all the orbs shone bright at the beginning, tell me, Child of Kharkhania - how many now lie in rest, their glow folded back into the earth?"

The golden letters flickered once, then sank into the bark, leaving faint trails of warmth in the air. Tiara's gaze lingered on the empty space where the riddle had hovered. The silence of the glade deepened - not empty, but waiting.

The Great Tree rustled faintly, as if it were leaning closer, listening for her answer.

(Can you figure out how many orbs lie dim at the end of the ritual - before Tiara does?)

Space for you, Thinker

Solution on page 186

The forest went completely quiet, as if waiting for what would happen next. Tiara called out the answer with full confidence. For a moment, everything stopped-then the air came alive. Thousands of leaves spun around the great tree, then around Tiara and Teksh in a circle of green light. The fifth piece of the Sapphire Cube rose gently from the hollow and joined the other pieces, fitting perfectly into place.

A wave of color spread across the world. The dark tree came alive again, glowing with light that changed with every breath Tiara took. When she breathed in, the light grew brighter; when she breathed out, warmth spread across the sky. It felt as if she and the tree were one, their hearts beating together with the life of this strange world.

The soft glow reached every corner of the forest. Flowers bloomed once more, their petals unfolding in colors she had never seen before. The rivers of light began to flow again, and the creatures that had hidden in fear slowly returned, circling the tree with quiet joy. Tiara felt a gentle happiness rise inside her-a sense that she had restored something sacred.

Then she understood. The piece of the cube she had taken no longer drained the life of this world because the forest and she had become one. The energy that once belonged to the tree now flowed through her. As long as Tiara lived, the forest would live too. It no longer needed the cube for strength; its magic had found a new home-within her heart.

Teksh looked up at her, eyes shining with pride. "You did it," his gaze seemed to say. Tiara smiled, brushing her hand against his soft fur. "We did it," she said happily.

Then the massive branches began to move, bending gently, pointing toward the hollow at the tree's core. Tiara understood-it was guiding them onward. The leaves rustled softly, almost like a goodbye. Bowing deeply in gratitude, she pressed her palms together and said, "Thank you."

The hollow glowed brighter, its light spinning in slow circles, pulling them closer. The air filled with the pulse of energy and the faint scent of rain and earth.

Tiara took one last look at the shining forest, her heart full of hope and courage for what waited ahead.

A gentle tremor ran through the ground, as if the whole forest exhaled in a soft blessing. Blue and gold lights rose from the soil and circled Tiara like tiny fireflies, brushing her skin with warmth. Teksh bowed his head, sensing the forest's quiet support. Tiara let the glow settle in her heart, steadying her resolve for the path ahead.

Without hesitation, she jumped into the glowing hollow and disappeared into the swirling light. Teksh let out a firm snort and followed her, diving straight into the heart of the living tree.

****

Chapter 10 – The Wizard's Trap (Puzzle VIII)

Tiara and Teksh fell through the tree as though sliding inside a long, glowing tunnel. The walls curved and twisted around them, filled with soft light that pulsed like a heartbeat. They couldn't tell if they were falling fast or drifting slowly-the feeling changed with every turn. The air was thick with voices and faint echoes, as if the tree itself was speaking in a language they couldn't yet understand.

After what felt like hours-or maybe only moments-they landed gently on solid ground. Tiara blinked, trying to steady herself. They were no longer inside the tree. Around them stretched a wide, flat land shaped like a perfect square, floating in the middle of a silent, endless void. There was no sky, no ground-only a soft golden haze that faded into nothingness.

They looked around, but there were no stars, no wind, not even shadows. Time felt lost here. Tiara couldn't tell how long they had been travelling or even which direction they had come from. Teksh pawed the glowing surface beneath them-it was smooth like glass but warm, as if alive.

Then the stillness broke. A faint vibration ran through the floating land, low and deep, like distant thunder. Tiara turned sharply, her eyes scanning the horizon. From the far edge of the platform, something began to take shape-a shadow rising slowly out of the golden mist.

The figure grew taller as it moved closer. He was nearly twice the height of any man Tiara had ever seen, wrapped in dark, flowing robes that shifted as though moved by an invisible wind. A wide hat hid most of his face, but beneath it, two piercing eyes glowed faintly-cold, sharp, and full of knowing. A long moustache hung from his face, twitching like living threads. In one hand, he held a dragon-shaped staff that glowed with a dull red light, and with ancient power."

The floating land trembled as the wizard struck his staff against it, sending a shower of sparks into the void. The sound rolled through the emptiness like a storm trapped inside the air itself.

When he spoke, his voice was calm but heavy, carrying a strange weight that made the air around Tiara and Teksh tremble.

"I am Chantrik, servant of Zarkasur," he said slowly. "You stand in the hollow of the Between World-the place where magic itself bends. Your strength, your courage... they mean nothing here. All that you carry will soon be dust."

Tiara's throat tightened. Even Teksh lowered his head and growled, the air pressing around them like invisible walls. Tiara forced herself to speak, her voice small but steady. "Why are you here? If you serve Zarkasur, then why don't you stop us now?"

Chantrik tilted his head slightly, his faint smile hidden beneath his hat. "Stop you?" he repeated softly. "Child, if I wished to end you, I could turn your breath to stone before your next heartbeat." His eyes flickered, and for a moment, the air around Tiara froze cold. Then, just as suddenly, it eased.

"But I am not a killer," he continued. "I am the master of paradox. I deal in the space between truth and illusion. My purpose is not to destroy you, but to show you what waits ahead-to make you understand what courage will cost you, and your world."

Tiara frowned, her fear giving way to confusion. "You sound like you don't want to serve him."

Chantrik let out a low laugh, echoing like cracked stone. "Want? There is no 'want' left in me. I was a keeper once, before Zarkasur tore my soul from its light and bound it to his will. Now I am both servant and prisoner-free to speak, but never to choose."

He stepped closer, his voice deepening. "Every brave act burns bright for a moment, but every light feed on something to stay alive. You will learn this soon, you will see what your courage consumes."

Tiara took a step back, her heart pounding, but she didn't look away. The mark on her forehead glowed faintly. "We will never let our world fall," she said quietly. "Not while I still breathe."

Chantrik's smile grew thin. "Then breathe deeply, child," he said. "For breath itself is borrowed time."

He lifted his staff, and red sparks swirled around him. The air cracked, filling with murmurs that weren't quite words. "Go," he said at last. "The master awaits. I will not stop you-but I will see you again, when your light begins to fade."

His voice sank into the void like a fading echo. Then his body turned to drifting dust, leaving behind a trail that curled through the air:

"It is destined – a light must face its shadow."

For a long moment, nothing moved. The air was still, heavy with the echo of his words. Tiara stood frozen, staring at the place where Chantrik had vanished. Her heart raced, but the mark on her forehead glowed softly, calming her trembling hands.

Teksh stepped closer, his hooves clinking gently against the glowing surface. He looked at her, his deep eyes steady, full of silent strength. Tiara reached out and rested her hand on his neck. "We keep going," she says. "No matter what waits ahead."

Slowly, the ground beneath them began to vibrate again. The floating platform shuddered, then started to sink through the air, moving gently but surely downward. Around them, the golden mist thickened, folding in like soft waves. The silence returned-but this time, it felt like the calm before something greater.

The vast square of land drifted lower through the glowing emptiness. Tiara and Teksh stood close together, watching quietly as it moved through the mist. Below them, a narrow path of light appeared-just wide enough for the two of them to walk side by side. It stretched far into the distance, fading into the haze like a bridge between worlds.

At last, the platform slowed and came to rest beside the glowing path. The air was still again, heavy and charged with quiet energy. Tiara looked down into the endless void on either side, then turned to Teksh. He met her gaze and nodded once, his eyes calm but alert.

Without a word, they stepped onto the narrow path, their journey continuing into the unknown.

At the end of the path stood a door-dark red, smooth, and ancient.

There were no locks, no guards, no hinges-only strange symbols etched across its surface, glowing faintly like veins of molten gold.

Tiara stepped closer, tracing the carvings with her fingers. The patterns seemed alive, shifting subtly as if watching her.

"This must be it," she believed. "The next piece is behind this door."

Teksh tilted his head, studying the base of the door. His sharp eyes caught something Tiara had missed-a second, smaller row of markings running along the bottom edge, half-hidden in shadow.

"Tiara," he said softly, tapping the ground with his hoof, "look here... I think the real clue begins below."

As soon as her fingers brushed the symbols, light burst outward from the red door. The air rippled, and the two found themselves standing in a vast circular arena. The sand beneath their feet glowed with heat; banners of golden fire waved in a wind that wasn't there.

Around them, twenty-five spectral horses appeared - silver and translucent, each radiating its own faint aura. A voice rolled out from the door behind them, deep and echoing:

"These are the Stallions of Swift-run - twenty-five in all, none the same.

Five may race at a time upon the Tracks of Fire. You may not measure their speed by any clock - only by the order in which they finish. The stallions never change their true pace.

You may arrange the races as you wish, choosing who runs in each. Your task is to discover not only the fastest, but the three swiftest of all.

Tell me, Seeker - what is the least number of races you must run to know, with certainty, the top three?"

The voice fell silent. The spectral stallions pawed the glowing sand, their breath rising like mist.

The air trembled with the sound of distant hooves - waiting for Tiara's command.

(Can you figure out the fewest races needed to find the three fastest stallions before Tiara does?)

Space for you, Thinker *Solution on page 189*

Her final word echoed through the silence, and the symbols on the red door began to shift-turning, aligning, solving themselves - until a golden handprint emerged at the center, pulsing with light.

Understanding its message, Tiara raised her hand and pressed her palm against the mark. Instantly, warmth surged through her fingers. Streams of golden particles flowed from her palm into the door, racing across its surface like living light. The energy traced every edge, every line, until the entire frame glowed - and then, with a soft buzz, the door dissolved into thin air.

Beyond it floated the sixth piece of the Sapphire Cube, hanging in the air at Tiara's eye level, glowing softly like captured starlight. The air around it throbbed with light, as if the shard carried a heartbeat of its own.

Tiara hesitated for a moment, almost expecting it to test her like the others had - but the shard moved gently on its own, drifting toward her. It merged with the other pieces inside her pocket, fitting perfectly as though it had been waiting for its place all along.

The cube glowed brighter for a moment, pulsing softly. Then a new side appeared-etched with the image of a delicate compass. Its silver needle spun wildly at first, whirling in all directions before slowing down and coming to a stop. It pointed straight ahead, through the empty space where the door had just stood.

Tiara turned the cube slowly in her hands, watching the needle. No matter how she moved it, the compass refused to change direction. The needle stayed still, steady and sure, as if drawn by something powerful beyond sight.

A quiet breeze swept past, stirring her hair. The air ahead seemed to ripple faintly, like the edge of a dream. For a moment, Tiara felt the strange pull of the unknown-a feeling both heavy and inviting. Teksh stepped closer, his ears flicking, sensing it too.

She met his gaze, her eyes full of determination and wonder. "It's through there," she said softly. Her voice steady and carried a quiet strength.

Teksh nodded, his fur catching the faint glow from the cube. Together, they turned toward the unseen path that waited ahead-where the compass pointed, and destiny called.

****

Chapter 11 – The Desert of Dhatkidith (Puzzle IX)

The other side was breathtaking-a land of mist-clad mountains, silver waterfalls tumbling through clouds, twin rainbows arching across golden skies, and valleys blooming in endless colour.

For a moment, Tiara and Teksh stood silent, hearts swelling with emotion. The place reminded them of Bistaria-of Bhavam's laughter, Rivaaya's wisdom, and the warmth of their villagers. For an instant, it felt like home. But deep inside, they knew this was not it. Their real home was still in danger, and that thought only strengthened their resolve.

They had lost count of days. Tiara could only feel time pressing on her shoulders, heavy and silent, like a breath held too long. The compass needle, steady until now, pointed west-toward a vast jungle that glimmered beneath the rainbows.

Tiara and Teksh followed the trail, the forest canopy closing above them like a curtain of green light. Strange creatures peeked curiously from behind glowing leaves, their eyes reflecting magic and innocence alike.

The compass in Tiara's hand began to tremble. Its needle spun wildly, faster and faster, until it was just a blur of motion. Tiara stopped walking. "Something's wrong," she says, her voice barely louder than the wind.

They moved carefully, each step hesitant, the ground soft beneath their feet. The air felt different here-thicker, heavier. Teksh's ears twitched; he could sense something too.

Then Tiara stopped again. Her forehead creased. She stretched out a hand-and froze. There was nothing in front of her, yet her fingers met resistance, hard and cold.

She pressed gently. The air rippled faintly, like water disturbed by a drop of rain. "An invisible wall," she murmured.

They turned right. Another wall. Left-another. The path behind them, too, was gone. Within moments, the world had shrunk to a small, unseen cage.

The silence that followed was suffocating. Even the wind seemed to have vanished. Tiara could hear only the echo of her own breathing and the quick, nervous rhythm of Teksh's hooves shifting on the ground.

Then, from above, came a sound-soft at first, then growing clearer. A low, echoing laugh rolled across the air, cold and hollow.

Tiara looked up. The sky above them distorted, twisting like glass under light. Out of that distortion stepped Chantrik. His cloak flowed slowly, waving against the air as if woven from shadows themselves. The dragon-staff in his hand glowed from within, a steady pulse beating like the heart of the void.

"You've come far, little one," he said, his voice smooth and dangerous. "But not far enough."

The light above their heads grew solid and spread downward, highlighting a structure around them. In moments, they were trapped inside a huge glass cage - clear, but filled with shifting reflections that seemed to move on their own.

Teksh pawed at the ground, snorted once, and lowered his head. He charged with all his strength, crashing into the invisible wall. The sound echoed like thunder, but the cage didn't even tremble. He tried again. And again. The thuds grew weaker, each one swallowed by the heavy silence.

"It's no use," Tiara tells finally. Her voice trembled as she touched Teksh's shoulder. "It won't break."

Tiara's pulse raced. Panic clawed at her chest-but beneath the noise of fear, something older stirred. A memory. Her mother's voice, calm and steady, echoed in her mind.

She had been five then, sitting by the river as fireflies blinked over Kharkhania's calm water. Rivaaya had cupped her small hands and gently says,

"Fear comes when we forget that the world breathes with us. Listen, Tiara. When you are scared, don't push the world away - feel it move through you."

She had touched Tiara's forehead gently, her fingers tracing the faint crescent.

"That is when the Horeksh will hear you. It listens not to strength, but to calm."

Tiara remembered the gentle murmur of the river that night, the glow of her mother's smile, the warmth of her palms. Even then, she had felt the rhythm-the quiet pulse between her heartbeat and the world's.

The memory steadied her trembling hands. She drew in a deep breath and lowered herself to the ground. The air around them seemed to hold its breath too.

She sat cross-legged, her palms resting gently on her knees. The glow from the glass walls flickered, uncertain. Tiara began to chant the ancient Horeksh Mantra - a song of balance and energy.

Her crescent birthmark began to glow-softly at first, then brighter, pulsing like a second heart. The light deepened, spreading across her face and spilling onto the walls, until the air itself seemed to hum with energy. The glass flashed, cracked, and finally shattered into a thousand glittering fragments that dissolved into the air.

The released energy swept across the land, calming the disturbed winds. Tiara bowed her head to the world around her. "Thank you," she whispered.

Chantrik hovered in stunned silence. He had underestimated the little girl. A mere child-yet she had broken his illusion. His eyes narrowed as he faded into smoke. "Impressive," his voice echoed, cold and distant. "But this is far from over."

The last fragments of the shattered dome drifted through the air like dust in moonlight. Tiara's breath came uneven, her palms still tingling from the energy of the Horeksh. Teksh stepped close, lowering his head, his warm breath brushing her arm.

High above, the air shimmered faintly. Though Chantrik had vanished, his presence lingered-like a shadow refusing to fade. The echo of his voice rippled through the silence, low and unsettling. Somewhere beyond sight, he was watching, learning, waiting.

Tiara looked down at the compass in her hand. Its needle quivered once, then stilled-pointing firmly ahead. She exchanged a quiet glance with Teksh. Whatever came next, it would not wait long.

They followed the needle into curling silver mist. The air thinned, silence deepened, and beneath it all was a faint pulse-steady, unfamiliar, alive.

At last, the mist parted, revealing a clearing unlike any they had seen before. Guided by the steady compass needle, Tiara and Teksh stepped forward into a strange arena.

The place felt different-silent and hollow. It was perfectly circular, its ground bare and lifeless, with no trace of flora or fauna. Yet around its edge, countless animals moved in a continuous circle-elephants, deer, birds, even serpents-each pacing in perfect rhythm, as if bound by an unseen spell. None dared to cross the boundary or step into the circle where Tiara and Teksh now stood.

A deep hush fell. The air thickened with anticipation. Tiara's heartbeat quickened; she could feel the weight of unseen eyes watching. Then, from the line of circling creatures, a tiger stepped forward-massive, striped with gold and black, its gaze burning with both intelligence and power.

As the tiger entered the circle, the other animals began to move faster, their steps turning into a silent rhythm. The tiger's strong body moved with power as it came closer, its golden eyes fixed on Tiara.

Without thinking, Teksh stepped in front of her. His hooves pressed hard into the ground, his body tense and ready to protect her. A low snort escaped him - a warning to the tiger. The air felt heavy, filled with silence and danger.

But the tiger didn't attack. It stopped a few steps away and looked from Teksh to Tiara, as if trying to understand something. Then, slowly, it lifted one large paw and began to draw on the ground - lines and shapes that crossed each other, forming glowing symbols in the dust.

The animals around the circle moved faster, their rhythm so steady it seemed to merge with Tiara's own heartbeat.

“The Desert of Dhatkidith,” tiger rumbled. “A place where reason and patience are worth more than gold.”

The glowing lines formed an image: a caravan at the edge of an endless desert, dunes stretching into the horizon. A single beast of burden stood beside three towering mounds of fruit-each glowing golden under the sun.

“Listen well, seeker,” said the tiger.

“A merchant once stood upon this very sand with three thousand sunfruits.

The market lies a thousand leagues away across the dunes.

His beast can carry no more than a thousand sunfruits at once. It eats one fruit per league it travels-whether forward or back.

The merchant may store fruits anywhere along the path, creating small storage spots for his return, but he may carry only a thousand at a time.

What is the greatest number of fruits he can deliver to the far market, a thousand leagues away, if he plans his journey perfectly?

The pattern pulsed with light. Tiara frowned. "It eats one for every league it takes-forward or back?"

The tiger nodded. "The wise traveller learns when to move and when to leave a store behind."

The lines of the puzzle blazed brighter, then faded, leaving only a single inscription in the dust:

He who hoards will empty his hands; he who parts with weight will reach the farthest shore.

Teksh leaned close, his voice low. "It's not just a riddle of distance-it's a riddle of balance. Move too far with too much, and you lose more than you gain."

Tiara closed her eyes, tracing invisible numbers on her palm. "So that's what he's testing," she mutters. "Patience and planning."

The tiger's eyes glimmered. "Then find your answer, seeker. The fate of this path may rest on it."

Tiara knelt beside it, staring at the puzzle etched into the ground. Her throat tightened. "What if I can't do this?" her voice trembling. One mistake… and Bistaria would fall.

Teksh nudged her arm gently, his warm gaze steady and sure. The quiet strength in his eyes anchored her. Tiara drew a long breath, feeling her heartbeat slow, her thoughts sharpen. When she opened her eyes again, the fear had melted into focus.

(Can you determine the maximum number of sunfruits that can reach the market, before Tiara does?)

Space for you, Thinker *Solution on page 192*

Tiara traced the glowing symbols with care. Each touch sent ripples of light across the pattern, spreading like waves on water. The warmth beneath her fingers felt alive - almost breathing.

Teksh stood close behind her, his calm presence steadying her. The animals around them had gone silent, their eyes shining in the faint glow. Even the air seemed to pause, waiting.

Tiara studied the symbols one last time. The answer felt right - not in her mind, but deep in her heart. Kneeling, she drew her answer beside the riddle in the dust.

A spark leapt across the pattern, sharp and bright. The ground answered with a low, resonant pulse, like a drum struck by the earth itself.

The tiger let out a low growl that built into a powerful roar - not of anger, but of pride and recognition. Its golden eyes softened, gleaming like twin suns. The markings on its body flared, breaking apart into glowing fragments that swirled in the air.

From its mouth burst a beam of golden light, pure and steady. The light gathered in the space before Tiara, swirling and tightening until it shaped itself into the seventh piece of the Sapphire Cube. It hovered in the air, radiant and weightless, then drifted forward and merged with the others in Tiara's pocket, pulsing gently as if welcoming its kin.

As it locked into place, the cube pulsed, and the third side appeared-an elegant hourglass, its golden sand trickling steadily downward. Tiara's chest tightened as the truth struck her. Every grain of sand was a heartbeat closer to the end.

Teksh pawed at the hourglass engraved on the cube, his expression tense. Only two days' worth of sand remained. Tiara watched in silence, the faint glow of the cube reflecting in her eyes. The weight of what lay ahead pressed against her chest, heavy but clear - the end was near.

The tiger no longer seemed fierce or frightening. Its eyes, once burning with power, now held warmth and quiet respect. The air around them thickened with stillness, the kind that feels sacred rather than silent.

The animals that had circled them moments ago stopped as if guided by a single thought. They turned inward, their eyes shining softly in the fading light. Then, slowly, each raised a paw, a hoof, or a wing - an ancient gesture of honour, graceful and wordless. A gentle wave of golden light swept through the clearing, brushing over Tiara's skin like warmth after a storm.

Teksh stood tall beside her, his chest rising with pride. Tiara felt a strange calm settle over her. These creatures weren't just bowing to her - they were trusting her, handing her their hope.

The tiger lowered itself, its great head dipping low in invitation. Tiara hesitated for a breath, then placed her hand on its striped mane. The fur was warm and smooth beneath her fingers. She climbed onto its back, her heartbeat steadying as she met the creature's gaze.

With a mighty leap, the tiger raced through the jungle, its stride silent and smooth as the wind. Leaves brushed past in streaks of green and gold. Teksh followed close behind, his hooves drumming against the earth in strong, rhythmic beats - the sound of faith chasing destiny.

****

Chapter 12 – The Temple of Light (Puzzle X)

They ran north until the trees grew thinner and the jungle opened into a wide clearing. Ahead, a river poured into a deep, dark hole that seemed to swallow all the light around it. The tiger stopped at the edge and turned to Tiara. Its golden eyes showed no fear, only trust. It gave her one final nod toward the water.

Tiara hesitated for a heartbeat, then took a deep breath. "Come on, Teksh," she encourages. Together, they dove in.

The river pulled them instantly downward, twisting and spinning through the dark tunnel. Water roared in their ears, and flashes of light-streaked past like shooting stars. After what felt like forever, they burst through the surface into a strange place.

They found themselves standing on a small cliff-like platform surrounded by a towering wall of mountains. A hundred waterfalls thundered from every direction, converging into a single cascade that crashed toward the centre where Tiara and Teksh stood. Mist filled the air, glittering like shards of crystal. Behind them, the den from which they had emerged had vanished - nothing remained but the roar of endless water.

The space was shrinking. The water rose quickly, swirling around their feet, their waists, their necks. But Tiara and Teksh did not panic-they had learned the art of breathing beneath water. Yet as the flood climbed higher, Teksh frowned. "Something's wrong," he said, his voice uneasy.

The water clung to their skin, thicker than before-sticky, heavy, almost alive. Tiara dipped her head below the surface and gasped. It wasn't just water-it was something else, a strange, viscous substance that refused to let them breathe. Panic sparked in her chest.

"We have to find a way out," she said urgently. Together, they scanned the swirling walls of water, searching desperately for an escape as the liquid world around them grew darker and tighter.

Through the dark, swirling water, a huge shadow began to move. The river shook as something enormous glided beneath them - a creature older than time. Slowly, it rose from the depths, breaking through the glowing water.

It was a giant serpent with a long, powerful body covered in blue-green scales that shone like glass. Soft light moved across its sides as its wide fins opened like wings. Its face was that of an owl-calm, noble, and wise. Golden feathers circled its glowing amber eyes, which seemed to hold the secrets of the world. When it looked at Tiara, the air itself grew still. It felt less like a beast and more like an ancient guardian, watching over the land and all its magic.

It circled them once, twice, then again, the motion creating powerful whirlpools that pulled Tiara and Teksh helplessly into its grasp. In an instant, its massive tail coiled around them, lifting both high above the water. The creature's voice rumbled through the water like thunder.

"Who dares enter my realm?" it boomed. "Who are you, and why have you come here? None who meet Lochnaag ever leave alive."

Tiara struggled to breathe but kept her voice steady. "We've come to save our home-Bistaria. We seek the pieces of the Sapphire Cube to defeat Zarkasur."

Lochnaag's laughter rolled across the chamber, deep and mocking, shaking droplets loose from the rocky ceiling. "Defeat Zarkasur?" he echoed, his eyes gleaming. "You are both brave... and foolish. Brave enough to reach this cursed depth - and foolish enough to think you can challenge the Lord of

Darkness himself. None escape my waters. I shall devour you and end your journey here!"

Tiara's breath caught, but she refused to step back. The glow from Lochnaag's scales painted ripples of blue and gold across her face. "If you wanted to end us," she said quietly, "you would have done it already." Her voice trembled, but her gaze did not waver. "So, what is it you really want?"

The serpent's vast head tilted slightly, and a sound-half hiss, half hoot-echoed through the cavern. "Clever little spark," he murmured. "Even at the edge of doom, you choose hope over fear." His coils shifted, stirring waves that crashed against the stone walls. "I do not crave your end, child of Bistaria. I crave understanding. And only those who can answer what the waters hide are worthy to rise again."

Teksh took a cautious step forward, the faint glow from the runes reflecting in his eyes. "Then test us," he said, his voice low but steady. "But know this-we will not turn away."

Lochnaag's coils glowed brighter, casting ripples of light across the rising water. The runes along his body began to shift and twist, moving like living streams of fire. Tiara watched in awe as the glowing patterns lifted from his scales and spread across the misty air above them. The lights swirled together, shaping themselves into a grand vision-a vast temple hanging in the sky, its floor made of glass and flame. The image hovered there, bright and alive, until it seemed less like magic and more like a memory of another world-real and waiting.

Within the glowing vision, the temple's heart came into focus. A hundred candles burned in a perfect circle, their flames steady and golden. Before each flame stood a cloaked figure-silent, unmoving, watching the eternal fire. The light wavered, and from the depths of Lochnaag's scales rose a voice, calm and deep as distant thunder.

"Behold the Temple of Light.

Inside it stand a hundred guardians, each watching over a single sacred flame. Every guardian can see the brightness of every other flame, but not the flame of their own.

Each one is wise and logical, and they all know that the others are just as logical as they are. There are no mirrors in this temple, no reflections on glass. They live by one vow:

If ever a guardian becomes certain that their own flame burns, they must extinguish it at dawn and leave the temple forever.

All dawns are shared - every departure seen by all. One night, a lone wanderer climbed the temple steps. From the threshold he spoke aloud so every guardian could hear:

'At least one flame among you burns brightly.'

The words were small, and yet they set thought ablaze. For in that instant, the fire's truth was no longer silent sight, but knowledge known to all. The wanderer's words echoed through the temple, so every guardian knew that every other had heard them too. After that, the wanderer turned and left.

The first dawn came-none moved.

The second dawn-stillness.

On and on the days passed, dawn after dawn, until at last the fateful dawn arrived.

One by one, waiting guardian stepped forward to the circle's edge, cupped their hands around their flame, and snuffed it out.

In perfect unison, the chosen guardians left the temple together as the sky blazed with gold."

The vision dissolved, its final light tracing across Lochnaag's scales before fading into quiet stillness.

(Can you figure out how many days will pass, and how many guardians will leave the temple, before Tiara does?)

Space for you, Thinker *Solution on page 195*

Tiara's pulse quickened. "They could see the light in others," she mumbles, "but not their own. So, they waited... waited until they were sure that everyone knew the light was seen."

Her reflection glowed faintly on Lochnaag's scales - her own courage staring back at her. In that moment, she understood. The riddle wasn't just about the guardians. It was about her... and everyone who forgets to see their own glow.

How often, she thought, do we notice the light in others - their strength, their hope, their courage - yet fail to see the same flame within ourselves? The truest light was never out there in the circle. It was within, quiet and waiting, until we dare to believe it burns.

The riddle was tough - perhaps the most intricate challenge in all of creation. Symbols twisted, water currents shifted, and even the light itself seemed to deceive. But Tiara was no ordinary mind. The gift of clarity and insight from her mother guided her every move. Every riddle she had ever solved, every test she had overcome, echoed within her now. With patience as her compass, she pieced together the meaning hidden across Lochnaag's scales.

The great serpent roared and twisted in anger, its coils turning the water into wild spirals. Then, in a flash of blinding light, its body broke apart into mist and disappeared, leaving behind complete silence.

The raging water began to sink and swirl away until it was gone. The ground cracked and dried beneath them, changing into a wide, bright plain under the sun.

From the very centre of the wasteland, a beam of Sapphire light erupted. The eighth shard of the cube emerged, gleaming like a captured star. It floated toward Tiara, spinning faster and brighter before merging with the larger cube in her hands. A new side appeared-this one carved with the image of a monstrous face and a blazing star.

Tiara's brow furrowed. The symbols were strange yet familiar. The monstrous face seemed fierce and dark, but the star beside it burned with quiet warmth.

Together, they felt neither good nor evil-just... balanced, as if one could not exist without the other.

She studied the cube closely, but its deeper meaning slipped beyond her grasp. It felt important-too vast to understand now, as though the truth behind it would reveal itself only when the time was right.

Her gaze lingered on the cube, memories stirring with its soft glow - doors that tested choice, storms that demanded courage, riddles that taught patience and trust. Each challenge had shaped her, every moment guiding her toward something greater. Even this new side-darkness and light carved as one-was part of a truth she was only beginning to see.

She turned the cube slowly, its surfaces gleaming in the dim light. Four faces now shone - Heart, Compass, Hourglass, and the Star with the Demon's visage - but two sides still waited, incomplete and silent. The final shard had yet to be found, and until it was, the cube - and their fate-would remain unfulfilled.

But there was no time to think. The hourglass on the cube had begun to glow brighter, its golden sand slipping through the narrow neck like a storm of time itself. Each grain fell, sharp and quick, echoing in Tiara's chest like a heartbeat. Teksh stood close, his breathing unsteady, watching the countdown that neither of them could stop. Only one day remained.

Yet no night had come for what felt like forever. The sky hung in a pale, endless light-draining, cold, and wrong. The air carried a strange stillness, as if the world itself had forgotten how to rest. Tiara's pulse quickened; a chill crept down her spine, reaching the edges of her thoughts. Time itself was breaking, and somewhere far above, it seemed, something-or someone-was controlling its flow.

****

Chapter 13 – The Architect of Paradox (Puzzle XI)

The compass in her hand began to spin wildly, faster and faster, exactly as it had before Chantrik's illusionary prison. Tiara's heart pounded. "Not again," she was infuriated.

The sky turned dark. The wind roared. Then, with a loud sonic tremor, a clear sphere of energy closed around them. Blue flames flickered in the air as the ground beneath their feet disappeared.

At the top of the sphere, floating like a dark star, appeared Chantrik-his dragon-staff glowing with a dull red light.

"Welcome back, little solver," his voice thundered.

The sphere shook and shot upward-through the clouds, beyond the stormy skies, higher and higher-until the world below turned into a blur of shadow and light.

Now they were floating in the endless silence of space. Beneath them, the Earth glowed blue and green, small and fragile in the darkness. Tiara could see Bistaria as a faint patch of light, its magic no longer pure. Streams of blue energy flowed from every forest, river, and creature, all being pulled into Zarkasur's dark and monstrous form.

Tiara's heart tightened. Through the glowing mist, she saw Bhavam leading the villagers, standing brave and strong to protect their home. Nearby, Rivaaya stayed with the frightened animals, her calm voice easing their fear. But above them, Zarkasur's laughter filled the sky, and Tiara felt her world slowly falling apart-its light fading bit by bit.

Inside the glowing sphere, Tiara and Teksh floated helplessly. They pushed, shouted, and even tried to use magic, but the barrier did not break. Tiara closed her eyes and chants the Horeksh Mantra, the same mantra that once summoned light and shattered glass. But this time, nothing happened. The air around them stayed still, heavy, and unyielding.

Then, from above, a low, mocking laugh echoed through the silence.

Chantrik appeared, floating effortlessly in the air, his dark cloak drifting like smoke. The dragon-staff in his hand pulsed like fire through stone, and his eyes gleamed with cruel pride.

"Your mantras cannot break this one," he said. "The Servikal Seal is my greatest creation-a spell strong enough to trap even the gods."

Tiara floated in the trembling air, her reflection twisting across the curved walls of the sphere. Every breath felt heavy, as though even the air now obeyed him.

Chantrik's laughter faded into a chilling calm. The space around him rippled-light bending, sound thinning-until it felt as if the world itself leaned toward his will. His presence pressed against Tiara's mind like a weight, silent yet overwhelming, as if reality had decided to listen only to him.

Tiara clenched her fists, the crescent mark on her forehead glowing faintly. "You're evil," she said, her voice trembling but firm. "You destroy worlds. You play with lives. You call that magic?"

Chantrik tilted his head, the faintest smile curling on his lips. "Evil?" he echoed, as though tasting the word. "Yes, perhaps. But every creation needs a shadow. Without me, there would be no balance-no puzzles for you to solve, no strength for you to find."

He lifted his staff, and the sphere trembled. "I am the greatest sorcerer in the universe," he said, his voice rolling like thunder. "The forest, the sea, the lands you crossed-every puzzle, every illusion-they were all my creations."

The staff spun slowly, and the air quivered like glass. Around them, ghostly visions flickered to life-the rising waterfall, the burning island, the golden door-all fading and reappearing like reflections on restless water.

"I control the rhythm of your world," he continued. "I can create days-or erase nights. While you solved riddles, I stole your time." His eyes glinted with strange delight. "I am not merely the Master of Magic… I am the Architect of Paradox."

Tiara's breath caught, but she met his gaze. "If you control everything," she said, "then why am I still standing against you?"

For a moment, Chantrik said nothing. The silence between them felt alive, stretched thin across the vibration of the sphere. Then, slowly, his smile returned-no longer mocking, but thoughtful.

He tilted his head slightly. "Courage and wit," he murmured. "A rare mix. In all my worlds, across centuries, no one-*no one*-has solved my riddles as you have. You were never meant to reach this far, child, yet here you stand."

His tone softened, almost admiring. "At such a young age, you hold more intelligence and bravery than the kings and sorcerers who came before you. You've earned my respect."

Then, his eyes hardened again, the warmth fading into ice. He lowered his staff, and its glow deepened to crimson fire.

"But respect does not grant mercy," he said. "It earns a final test. One question-the hardest of all. Answer it, and I will let you fight for your world's survival. Fail..." His voice deepened into a growl. "And every trace of your magic, your family, your people-will vanish into eternal silence."

Tiara's pulse pounded in her ears. Fear pressed against her chest, but she forced it down. Her gaze steadied.

"Ask it," she said quietly. "Ask your question, Chantrik. I'm ready."

Chantrik's eyes gleamed like chips of coal. He spoke slowly:

"There is a prison of one hundred souls. Each is held alone in a cell. One Test awaits them all-and once it begins, no voice may pass between them.

In the centre lies an interrogation chamber with a single lamp-one tiny light that can be switched on or off.

The wardens will bring each soul, one at a time, into that chamber in an order none can predict. No one can ever see who was taken before them, who will come after, or who enters at any other time. Each visit is silent and unseen. When a soul steps inside, they may choose to toggle the lamp - or leave it untouched. They never know when they will be brought again, nor how often.

At any moment, any soul may stand and declare: 'All one hundred have visited the lamp-room at least once.' If that declaration is true, freedom follows. If it is false, doom falls upon them all.

The souls may meet once before the test, to plan. After that, no word may be passed.

Tell me: what plan will they agree upon so that, eventually, they can be certain and declare that all have been there at least once?"

The light from Chantrik's staff dimmed to a cold white glow. Shadows stretched across the floor, like the bars of an unseen cage.

Tiara stood very still. Her thoughts darted like fish through deep water - a hundred silent souls, a single lamp, no voice between them. One word could end it all. One choice could set them free-or destroy them forever. But how could anyone ever know for certain?

She closed her eyes. The rules turned in her mind - the silence, the signal, the patience required. The answer was there, hidden beneath logic and time.

(Can you figure out the plan the souls made before the test begins, before Tiara does?)

Space for you, Thinker

Solution on page 199

It was not easy-perhaps the hardest puzzle in the universe. Tiara's heart pounded, her mind racing, yet clarity bloomed at the last moment. She called out the answer, her voice steady with conviction. For a long beat, Chantrik's stern face did not change. Then, slowly, he lowered his staff.

A thin smile tugged at his moustache. "No one has ever solved it," he murmured, almost in awe. "Power may be broken, but riddles-riddles are truth. And truth must be honoured."

He paused, his eyes softening as if he were looking far beyond her. "Do you know, child, why riddles exist? They are the shape of life itself. We are all caught inside them-every moment, every choice. We move from one riddle to the next, small or great, each one teaching us something before we pass to another. No one escapes them-not kings, not gods, not even me."

The faint glow of his staff flickered. "That is why I test, and why I respect those who dare to solve. For every answer found is a piece of truth reclaimed."

His body began to unravel, fading like ash carried by a quiet wind. As he vanished, his final words lingered, woven with both warning and wisdom:

"This isn't over. Every ending hides its next riddle, and life will make sure you find it."

The dragon-staff shrank, glowing, transforming into the final shard of the Sapphire Cube. One by one, the other pieces floated from Tiara's pouch and locked into place, the cube whole at last.

The fragments rose into the air, each glowing with its own hue. Streams of light arched between them, weaving together like threads of living fire. Sparks leapt and danced in perfect rhythm, drawing the pieces closer until they merged into one.

The air around Tiara glowed. The cube began to pulse, its light deepening from soft blue to blinding white. It spun faster, the vibration deepening into a low, resonant song that filled the void. With a final burst of light, it sealed itself-whole, perfect, complete.

A flawless Sapphire Cube now hovered before her, radiant and alive with limitless energy. Four faces glowed with symbols - Heart, Compass, Hourglass, and the Demon & Star.

But when Tiara turned it slowly in her palms, she saw that two new sides had also appeared. They were perfectly smooth, blank, untouched by any mark or image. The light around them flickered faintly, as if waiting for something still to come.

Tiara's breath caught. She could feel it - the cube was complete, yet unfinished. It was powerful, yet patient. The last two sides seemed to mumble a secret beyond sight, a promise the universe had not yet spoken.

The glow pressed softly against her skin, and she felt as though the cube was listening - to her pulse, her fears, her hope.

The cube's light swelled until it filled the air around them, spilling outward in waves that touched everything - the stars, the skies, the farthest edges of creation. The light carried voices, faint and ancient, like echoes from forgotten worlds.

For a moment, Tiara saw glimpses - faces of beings she had never met, worlds that had long turned to dust, and rivers that glowed with the same turquoise fire as Kharkhania. It was as if all creation had paused to watch her, the small girl who had gathered light from darkness.

Teksh stood beside her, the reflections of the cube dancing in his eyes. "It's calling to the magic that binds all worlds," he murmured softly, almost afraid to break the silence. Tiara nodded.

Above Bistaria, through the torn clouds and blazing light, Zarkasur stirred. He had felt the cube's pulse before, but this was different. The sky itself trembled with its power. He could feel it now-the Sapphire Cube stood fully assembled, its power unbound.

His crimson eyes opened slowly, glimmering with irritation and unease. A cynical smile crept across his monstrous face-the kind that twisted hope into mockery. He knew the child had done it; the Cube had awakened, its light restored after millennia. But that knowledge didn't trouble him. No mortal, not even the chosen, knew how to awaken what lay sealed within.

The Sapphire Cube was power beyond understanding - raw, ancient, and locked behind truths lost to time. Let them hold it, he thought, for in their hands it was nothing more than a jewel. His smile deepened, cold and certain. Even destiny, it seemed, still played by his rules.

Far beyond the upper skies of Bistaria, the sphere around Tiara and Teksh flared once without warning- and shattered like glass. They fell together, a dying star-bright, burning, and uncertain if they would ever rise again.

The world spun into motion again. Wind screamed past them, colours and sound blurring together as they plunged through the endless sky toward Bistaria.

The land below grew larger, brighter, alive - waiting for its fate to unfold.

And as Tiara clutched the cube close to her chest, she made a silent vow - that even if the cube demanded everything, she would not let her world fall into shadow again.

****

Chapter 14 – The River's Final Song

Teksh looked up, his eyes fierce and unwavering. He gestured with a quick nod, signalling Tiara to climb onto his back. She obeyed, clutching his soft golden fur as they streaked through the clouds, chasing the last hope that still burned above Bistaria.

As they fell, Tiara's mind spun through memories: Zarkasur's arrival, the trembling of Kharkhania, Bhavam's brave smile, Rivaaya's wisdom, the riddles, the battles, the friends they lost-and the courage they found. Every moment that had shaped her now flashed before her eyes. She didn't know if they would survive, but she knew she wouldn't trade the journey for anything.

They looked like a shooting star to those below-a streak of sapphire and gold descending from the heavens. Teksh's body trembled under the force of the wind. He was thinking fast, his instincts sharper than ever. *I must protect her. No matter what.*

The ground rushed closer. Tiara could now see the dark, restless waters of the Kharkhania River-its glow long stolen by Zarkasur's shadow. Teksh gritted his teeth, straining every ounce of his magic to alter their fall. But he realized, in that instant, a heartbreaking truth-he couldn't save them both.

"Tiara!" he shouted, fighting the wind. "Kharkhania will catch you-go!"

With one final burst of strength, Teksh twisted his body, using the air currents to push Tiara toward the river. The thrust flung her safely toward the water-but sent him spiralling away into the dark.

Tiara screamed his name, but it was too late. Teksh hit the ground with tremendous force, the impact carving a deep crater into the earth. Dust and light exploded around him before everything went still.

Tiara plunged into Kharkhania's glowing waters. The river, alive with ancient magic, caught her gently. The waves turned soft as silk beneath her, glowing brighter where she touched them. The healing essence of the river flowed through her veins, easing every bruise, every ache, every fear.

She rose slowly from the luminous water, droplets cascading down her face like liquid stars. In both her hands, she held the Sapphire Cube, its six faces blazing with celestial light. As she stepped onto the riverbank, the world seemed to hold its breath.

Before her stood Bhavam, Rivaaya, the villagers, and the creatures of Bistaria-every soul she had fought to protect. They watched in silence, awe and hope reflected in their eyes. The fate of their world now rested on the small girl who had fallen from the sky.

Across the pink horizon stood Zarkasur, vast and terrible, his presence bending the very air. His voice rumbled like thunder.

"I am the most powerful being in the universe. I have already drained the magic from your land. In moments, Bistaria will fall silent forever. You cannot stop me - no one can."

Tiara's hands shook around the cube; her knees almost buckled. The mark on her skin burned, but she held firm. She was trembling-not from weakness, but from the crushing weight of what lay before her. All her life she had known only love, and now she faced the embodiment of fear itself. The cube's light pulsed in her hands, as though waiting for her choice.

Zarkasur's booming laughter filled the sky, shaking the very ground of Bistaria. "You may have the cube, child," he roared, "but you don't even know how to summon its power!" His colossal form swelled, eyes burning with cruel, mocking light.

Tiara tightened her grip on the cube, her voice quivering but steady. "Maybe not," she said, "but I know what you'll never understand-love."

Zarkasur sneered, his laughter cracking through the air like thunder. "Love is weakness. Power is all that lasts."

Tiara met his blazing eyes, the cube burning brighter between her hands. "That's where you're wrong," she said. "Power fades when it stands alone. But love-" her voice steadied, "love binds."

The cube pulsed once, alive with the strength of every soul in Bistaria. Tiara lifted her chin. "That's why you've already lost." Yet deep down, she was still trying to figure out how the cube could help her defeat Zarkasur.

Teksh lay motionless on the ground, his body still, his chest barely rising. Panic gripped her heart. She turned-and there stood Bhavam and Rivaaya, their faces calm yet heavy with love and understanding. They knelt beside her, wrapping their arms around their daughter.

"We're here," Bhavam whispered. "Whatever comes next, we face it together."

Tiara's eyes filled with tears. Around them, the villagers began to gather-men, women, and children; birds, deer, and even the river's gentle creatures. One by one, they came closer, forming a circle around Tiara and her parents. Without a word, they all embraced-

humans, animals, and nature united in one great heartbeat.

Then, something extraordinary happened.

From every forehead, a soft blue glow appeared-a thread of light, alive with magic. The strands rose like fireflies and flowed toward the Sapphire Cube in Tiara's hands. The cube absorbed each beam-the laughter of children, the loyalty of Teksh, the wisdom of Rivaaya, the courage of Bhavam, and the love of every living being in Bistaria.

"Magic is not about control, Tiara," her mother's voice echoed from memory. "It listens only to hearts that beat together."

The words struck her like a memory reborn. She saw herself as a child by the river, Rivaaya's hands guiding hers as they poured water into a bowl. "See how it moves?" her mother had said. "Every wave moves with the others - the small, the strong, and the still. They all flow together as one."

Tiara's breath caught. "That's it," she whispered. "It's never the power-it's the harmony."

At her words, the Sapphire Cube stirred in her palms. Its four radiant faces-Heart, Compass, Hourglass, and Demon & Star-flared to life, and then, at last, the two blank sides awakened.

New symbols bloomed where there had been silence: on one, a circle of interlocked hands, the mark of Unity; on the other, six converging rays of light forming a single shining chord-the mark of Harmony. For the first time, the cube was whole. It pulsed with a rhythm that matched the beating of her own heart-every soul in Bistaria joined as one.

Then the cube came alive with a low resonance, brighter and brighter, until it glowed like a small sun. One side-the one marked with a demon's face and a blazing star-came alive with fierce light. The two symbols turned slowly, locking into perfect alignment, as if the star was destined to strike the demon.

In that moment, Tiara understood. The cube was never meant to destroy-it was meant to restore balance. The star against the demon, good against evil, light against shadow. To seal Zarkasur, she had to unite them. Its true power was not born of spells or strength, but of love, unity, and the courage to face darkness with light.

Zarkasur's eyes widened as the cube flared with blinding brilliance. "No!" he roared. "You can't-!"

But Tiara had already moved. She rose to her feet, fire blazing in her eyes, her voice steady. "This is for Bistaria!"

With all her might, she hurled the glowing cube toward Zarkasur. It streaked through the air like a comet, leaving trails of blue fire. Just as Zarkasur opened his mouth to drain the world's final magic, the cube struck his forehead.

The world held its breath. Then, an explosion of light. The cube unfolded, its six sides opening like wings, each side glowing with ancient power. Electric streams of sapphire light surged out, wrapping around Zarkasur's body. He screamed, a sound that split the sky, his dark form thrashing as the cube's energy consumed him.

"No… not again… not after all these centuries!" he roared, his voice fading as the magic enclosed him. The cube tightened, sealing him within a cage of blinding light. The sky rippled, and with one final flash, both Zarkasur and the cube vanished-banished back to Sakaria for another ten thousand years.

The sky flared crimson one final time, then slowly softened, the colour bleeding away as Kharkhania's waters returned to their calm, turquoise radiance. The land exhaled-trees straightened, rivers sang again, and the life returned to the air, as though Zarkasur had never existed.

But Tiara saw none of it. Her gaze found only Teksh. She fell to her knees beside him. His chest barely moved, his breath shallow and fragile beneath her trembling hand. "No, Teksh... please don't leave me," she cries, her voice breaking on every word. Memories flooded her mind - his clumsy crashes into haystacks, his silly grin that followed, the fearless way he always stepped in front of danger for her. He was more than a friend, more than a sibling, more than a companion. He was a part of her very soul.

Bhavam stepped forward, his strong arms trembling as he lifted Teksh's motionless body. The crowd parted quietly, their eyes following him with unspoken fear. Step by step, he carried Teksh toward Kharkhania's glowing edge, where the water lay lit with a lunar glow.

The villagers followed in silence. Not a voice, not a breath - only the soft sound of the river waited with them. Rivaaya knelt beside the shore and pressed her palms to the surface. Her voice, barely more than a breath, began to weave an ancient hymn - the same one she had sung on the night they were blessed with their daughter's birth.

The sparkling light spread from her fingers and moved softly into the water. It flowed gently around Teksh's still body, wrapping him in ripples of silver and blue - as if the river itself reached out to hold him once more, the way a mother reclaims her child. The light deepened, the water stilled. Every heart leaned forward in hope. But nothing happened.

The glow dimmed. The air grew still. Seconds turned into minutes, each one heavier than the last. Tiara's heart ached with helplessness; she pressed her forehead to his neck, tears streaming freely.

Then-just as her tears touched the water - something stirred. A faint ripple broke across the surface. Teksh's ears twitched, his chest rose, and a soft sound escaped his throat. With great effort, he pushed himself upright, unsteady but alive.

A collective gasp swept through the crowd. Then cheers burst out-loud, wild, and full of tears. Tiara ran to Teksh and threw her arms around his neck, crying and laughing at the same time. "You're back," she whispered into his fur. "You're really back."

Teksh blinked, wobbled to his feet, and-true to himself-took two steps forward before crashing straight into a haystack. For a moment, everyone froze. Then laughter filled the air, louder than the river's song. Even Bhavam and Rivaaya smiled through their tears.

The river glowed softly beside them, its calm waves carrying the sound of joy. Tiara closed her eyes and breathed in the air of home-warm, alive, and full of magic once more.

She thought of everything they had faced-the puzzles, the storms, the times she had almost given up. She once believed that magic lived only in

Kharkhania's waters or in powerful objects like the cube. But now she understood-it lived in every choice, every act of courage and kindness.

And in that stillness, Tiara felt the river's secret - the quiet harmony of love and peace that holds the world together. Balance isn't found; it's created, when hearts move as one.

The sun dipped low, painting the world in gold. That evening, Bhavam and Rivaaya prepared a warm meal for Tiara and Teksh-the aroma of herbs and baked bread filling the air. It was not just food-it was comfort, love, and the quiet promise of tomorrow.

At night, under a sky scattered with silver stars, Tiara sat beside Teksh near the river's edge. The waters of Kharkhania shone with quiet grace, reflecting the calm light of the heavens-as if the river itself was resting after its long struggle. Tiara leaned against Teksh, her fingers tracing his golden fur. "We did it," she exclaimed, her eyes reflecting the starlight. Teksh gave a gentle snort, his warmth steady and comforting.

They sat there for hours, letting the night breathe around them-the first true night after so long. No stolen hours, no vanishing dusk-just the hush of wind through the trees, the gentle murmur of the river, and a sky that finally felt whole again.

Across the horizon, dawn began to break, painting the world in hues of gold and rose. The first light of morning touched Kharkhania's surface, turning it into a river of living diamonds.

Tiara smiled, feeling the rhythm of the world return - the dance of sunlight, the breath of life, the melody of home. She knew that new challenges might one day come, but for now, her heart was light.

Magic was safe. Love had won. And the story of Tiara and Teksh would live forever in the songs of Kharkhania's waves.

****

Epilogue – Where Magic Finds Its Home

Weeks passed, and peace returned to Bistaria. The villagers laughed again as they repaired their homes, planted new crops, and sang old songs together. The air that once felt heavy was now full of hope and life.

Tiara spent her days helping everyone in the village - fixing broken roofs, painting small wooden bridges, and replanting flowers near the paths. Teksh was always with her, carrying baskets of food or water. Sometimes he tripped and spilled everything, making everyone laugh again.

Bhavam and Rivaaya often watched her from a distance, smiling with pride. Their little girl had grown stronger and wiser. She had learned that real magic doesn't live in spells or stars - it lives in love, courage, and unity.

One evening, the temple bell rang again - clear and bright after many quiet weeks. Lanterns glowed across the village, and Kharkhania's waters sparkled under the moonlight. By the riverbank, the small boy's wooden boat floated upright once more, steady and shining in the gentle current. The river sounded alive again, as if singing in joy.

Later one evening, Tiara was putting away the few things she had kept from her journey - the silver ring, her keeper's belt, and a handful of memories too precious to part with. But when her hand brushed against the belt, she suddenly froze.

"The jar," she whispered. *"Biraksha... I left him in it."*

Her fingers moved to the spot where the enchanted jar had once been. The belt hung open - no jar, no weight, only a few silver grains of dust glimmering faintly, like the last trace of a spell fading away.

Tiara turned toward the horizon, where the river met the sea. The wind had fallen still, as if the world were staring at something - and trying to say something. For a long moment, she listened - to the silence, to the faint murmur of the waves, to the whisper of something unseen.

"Strange," she said softly. *"Or maybe... not."*

Far away, beneath the moonlit shore, a faint gleam stirred beneath the sand. The magical jar lay half-buried; its surface cracked with faint veins of blue light.

The evening wind blew softly. From behind a sand dune, a coil of smoke rose - dark and slender, shaping itself into a small dragon, translucent and silent. Its eyes glowed the same dull red as the staff once carried by Chantrik.

The smoky creature hovered above the jar. The air trembled as its claws, more shadow than substance, gripped the lid. A soft twist, a quiet click, and the seal broke.

A single thread of black mist escaped, curling into the twilight sky before vanishing. The river breeze carried it away, leaving only the jar, open and empty, half-submerged in the sand.

To be continued…?

****

Appendix – Solutions

Tiara's adventure in Nautica includes eleven puzzles, each testing logic and reasoning in a different way.

The first two puzzles - The Cave of Two Doors and The Golden Door - are gateway puzzles. They don't contain any part of the Sapphire Cube but test Tiara and Teksh's intelligence and courage to prove they are worthy of the real quest.

After these come nine main puzzles, each guarding a piece of the Sapphire Cube. Solving them teaches an important lesson and brings Tiara one step closer to restoring balance to her world.

Below are all eleven puzzles in order, along with their simple explanations and solutions.

The Cave of Two Doors (Puzzle I)

To open the Forbidden Cave, Teksh had to outsmart both guardians.
He chose one guard-let's call him Guard X-and asked: "If I asked the other guard whether Door A *(assume any door as door A)* leads to the way forward, would he say yes?"
Then Teksh simply did the opposite of the answer he got.

<u>Reasoning:</u>
No matter whom Teksh asked-the truth-teller or the liar-the answer would always come out opposite to the truth.

<u>*Case I – Teksh asked the guard who always tells the truth*</u>
This truthful guard will tell what the lying guard would say. The lying guard would have lied about whether Door A leads to the way forward.
So, even though the truthful guard speaks honestly, his answer reflects the liar's false reply. Hence, the answer Teksh receives is incorrect or flipped.

Case II – Teksh asked the guard who always lies

This lying guard will lie about what the truthful guard would have said. The truthful guard would have given the correct answer, but the lying guard reverses it.
So again, the final answer Teksh receives is incorrect or flipped.

Thus:

- If the guard answered "yes," then Door A was not the way forward.
- If the guard answered "no," then Door A was the way forward.

Final Answer:

Ask either guard: "If I asked the other guard whether Door A leads to the way forward, would he say yes?" Then do the opposite of their answer.

The Riddle of the Golden Door (Puzzle II)

The riddle speaks of three flames living under one roof. Their multiplied strength means the sparks of each flame merge into a single brightness-and that number is thirty-six.

Their total light ("counted one by one") means the three brightnesses added up to a single value - the mysterious "number known to the traveller."

The key line says the traveller knew that total, but was still unsure which flame was which. This means that more than one set of three flames could both "multiply" to thirty-six & "add" to the same total.

Let's imagine all the ways three positive numbers could "multiply" to form thirty-six:

- 1 × 1 × 36 → total = 38
- 1 × 2 × 18 → total = 21
- 1 × 3 × 12 → total = 16
- 1 × 4 × 9 → total = 14
- 1 × 6 × 6 → total = 13
- 2 × 2 × 9 → total = 13
- 2 × 3 × 6 → total = 11
- 3 × 3 × 4 → total = 10

Notice something special:

Two different groups - (1, 6, 6) and (2, 2, 9) - both "add up" to 13.

That's why the traveller couldn't decide even after knowing the total glow; both sets looked possible.

But the final clue solves it:

"Until the eldest began her chant."

That meant there was one flame set apart - one whose light rose higher, its chant stronger than the rest.

In the group (1, 6, 6), the two brightest flames are equal - there's no single eldest. In the group (2, 2, 9), one flame clearly shines brightest.

Thus, the correct trio is 2, 2, and 9.

Answer Summary:

- "Joined strength" → multiplication = 36
- "Total light" → addition = same number (13)
- Only one clear eldest → 2, 2, and 9

The three flames burn with brightness 2, 2, and 9.

Where Rivers Rise (Puzzle III)

Tiara pictured the bridge and the four travelers in her mind:

Traveler	Nature	Time to cross
A	The Swift One	1 heartbeat
B	The Shadow Walker	2 heartbeats
C	The Steady One	7 heartbeats
D	The Burdened One	10 heartbeats

At max two could cross at a time, moving at the pace of the slower traveler. The flame had to be brought back after each crossing.

Tiara thought carefully - if the slowest two crossed together, it would save far more time than pairing each of them with the faster ones. The key was to let the quicker travelers carry the torch back wisely.

Here's how she planned it:

1- A and B cross first → 2 heartbeats (A & B now on far side). A return with the flame → +1 heartbeat (total 3).

2- C and D cross together → +10 heartbeats (total 13).
B returns with the flame → +2 heartbeats (total 15).

3- Finally, A and B cross again → +2 heartbeats (total 17).

Just as the seventeenth heartbeat struck, the last traveler stepped onto solid ground - all four safely across.

Answer Summary:

Order of crossing -
(1) A & B cross → (2) A returns → (3) C & D cross → (4) B returns → (5) A & B cross again.

Total time: 17 heartbeats.

The Trial of the Flames (Puzzle IV)

The sentinel's riddle was one of logic, not luck. Tiara had to find the fewest souls needed to identify the cursed goblet among a thousand, knowing that the curse reveals itself only after a day - so each soul could test only once.

She realized each soul's fate (glow or fade) could act as a signal- a way to record information.

If a soul's essence dimmed, is marked as "1" and if their light endured, as "0," then each soul, through its state of glow or fading, adds one "place" in a code.
With two possible outcomes per soul (like a binary number), the total number of distinct patterns that can be formed is:
$2 \times 2 \times 2 \ldots$ (once for each soul) → or simply 2^n possible combinations.

Each pattern could represent a different goblet. So Tiara needed just enough souls for these combinations to cover all 1,000 goblets.

She counting softly to herself:

- $2^9 = 512 \rightarrow$ not enough.
- $2^{10} = 1{,}024 \rightarrow$ enough to cover every goblet.

That meant ten souls could uniquely identify one cursed goblet among a thousand - because their combined fates after the sun's turn would reveal a unique pattern pointing to the single cursed goblet.

Final Answer:

- Each soul can represent one "place" in a pattern of glow or fading.
- Ten souls ($2^{10} = 1{,}024$) create enough unique patterns to cover all 1,000 goblets.
- After one day, the arrangement of enduring and dimmed lights reveals the cursed goblet.

The Aether Egg (Puzzle V)

When the Aether Egg opened its riddle to Tiara, it revealed that two numbers were chosen, and their multiplied strength could be either 8 or 16.

Through the silhouettes' dialogue, each statement of uncertainty slowly uncovered the truth - until only one possibility remained.

Tiara began to reason through the pattern.

If their multiplied strength was 8, the possible pairs were (1, 8), (2, 4), (4, 2), (8, 1).

If their multiplied strength was 16, the possible pairs were (1, 16), (2, 8), (4, 4), (8, 2), (16, 1).

Total combinations: Nine.

Each silhouette knew only their own number. Their exchange of "I don't know" narrowed the field with every round.

(1) First exchange

"I don't know your number."

If the first silhouette had 16, it would instantly know that the second's number must be 1, as only one such combination exists - (16, 1).

Since the first silhouette doesn't know the number for sure, **(16, 1)** is ruled out.

(2) Second exchange

"I don't know your number."

If the second silhouette had 16, it would instantly know that the first's number must be 1, as only one such combination exists - (1, 16).

Also, if the second silhouette had 1, it would instantly know that the first's number must be 8, as only one such combination exists - (8, 1) - after the elimination of (16, 1) in the first round.

Since the second silhouette doesn't know the number for sure, **(1, 16)** and **(8, 1)** are ruled out.

(3) Third exchange

"I don't know your number."

If the first silhouette had 8, it would instantly know that the second's number must be 2, as only one such combination exists - (8, 2) - after the elimination of (8, 1) in the second round.

Also, if the first silhouette had 1, it would instantly know that the second's number must be 8, as only one such combination exists - (1, 8) - after the elimination of (1, 16) in the first round.

Since the first silhouette doesn't know the number for sure, **(8, 2)** and **(1, 8)** are ruled out.

(4) Fourth exchange

"I don't know your number."

If the second silhouette had 8, it would instantly know that the first's number must be 2, as only one such combination exists - (2, 8) - after the elimination of (1, 8) in the third round.

Also, if the second silhouette had 2, it would instantly know that the first's number must be 4, as only one such combination exists - (4, 2) - after the elimination of (8, 2) in the third round.

Since the second silhouette doesn't know the number for sure, **(2, 8)** and **(4, 2)** are ruled out.

(5) Final exchange – "Now I know your number."

Now only two possible combinations remain after the fourth statement: (4, 4) and (2, 4).

In both combinations, the number 4 of the second silhouette is common.

Hence, the first silhouette can be sure that the second silhouette's number is **4**.

Final Answer:

The number of the second silhouette is **4**.

	1st Silhouette	**2nd Silhouette**	**Multiplication**	**Elimination in Round**
S. No.	**1 S**	**2 S**	**1 S x 2 S**	**"I Don't know"**
1	16	1	16	I
2	1	16	16	II
3	8	1	8	II
4	8	2	16	III
5	1	8	8	III
6	2	8	16	IV
7	4	2	8	IV
8	4	4	16	Possible
9	2	4	8	Possible

Whispers of the Drowned (Puzzle VI)

Tiara realized this puzzle wasn't about trust or kindness-it was about reason and greed. Each mariner cared most about himself first, then about gold, and only then about hurting others.

To survive, the leader had to offer just enough gold to win specific number of votes-and no more.

She pictured the five mariners sitting around a table, their faces lit by the glow of scattered coins. To keep track, she named them A, B, C, D, and E. A was the leader, sitting at the head of the table. If A fell, B would become the new leader, then C, then D, and finally E.

In her mind, they began to disappear one by one into the dark sea, until only one of them remained.

Step 1 - Only E left

If only E remains, he takes all 100 coins.

(There is no one to share with.)

Step 2 - D and E left

D is leader. With 2 people, the leader needs 1 vote (his own) to pass, so D keeps 100 and E gets 0.

Step 3 - C, D, E left

C is leader and needs 2 votes (his own + one more). If C dies, we go to the 2-person case where D keeps 100 and E gets 0.

So, E would rather take 1 coin now than get 0 later. D would prefer C to die (so D can keep 100). Therefore C buys E with 1 coin, and keeps 99 for himself.

(Distribution: C = 99, D = 0, E = 1)

Step 4 - B, C, D, E left

B is leader and needs 2 votes (his own + one more). If B dies, the C-plan gives C = 99, D = 0, E = 1. Who gets 0 in that future? D gets 0.

So, D would accept 1 coin now rather than 0 later. C (who would get 99 later) will not accept 1. B offers 1 coin to D and keeps 99.

(Distribution: B = 99, C = 0, D = 1, E = 0)

Step 5 - A, B, C, D, E (full council)

A is leader and needs 3 votes (his own + two others). Look one step ahead to B's plan (if A dies): B = 99, C = 0, D = 1, E = 0.

Who would get nothing under B? C and E would get 0. Those two will gladly take a single coin now rather than get nothing later.

So, A bribes C with 1 coin and E with 1 coin, securing their votes. A keeps the rest:

100 − 1 − 1 = 98.

Final distribution: A = 98, B = 0, C = 1, D = 1, E = 0

Final answer:

The leader (A) can safely keep 98 coins. He gives 1 coin each to C and E to secure their votes, and the other two get nothing.

The Dwarfs of Kadmirah (Puzzle VII)

The Great Tree spoke of one hundred hollows beneath its roots. In each hollow lay a glowing orb of dawn, and at first, all were bright.

Then came the hundred dwarfs of Kadmirah, each numbered from 1 to 100.

The first dwarf touched every orb.
The second touched every second orb - 2, 4, 6, 8 …
The third touched every third - 3, 6, 9, 12 …
And so it went, until the hundredth dwarf touched only the last orb.

Each time a dwarf touched an orb, its glow changed - bright turned to dim, and dim to bright.

When the final dwarf stepped away, the forest fell silent. The Tree's voice lingered in the air:
"How many orbs now rest in the dark beneath my roots?"

Let's look carefully at what happens.

Orb 1 is touched only once - by the first dwarf - so its state changes one time. It started bright, and after one touch, it becomes dim.

Orb 2 is touched by two dwarfs - numbers 1 and 2. First bright → dim (after the first dwarf), then dim → bright (after the second). Two touches bring it back to bright again.

Orb 3 is touched by dwarfs 1 and 3 - two touches again - so it ends bright.

Orb 4 is special. It's touched by dwarfs 1, 2, and 4 - three touches. That's an odd number of changes, so it ends dim.

If you look at all the orbs, a pattern appears: most are touched an even number of times and stay bright, but a few are touched an odd number of times and end dim.

Those special orbs sit in hollows numbered 1, 4, 9, 16, 25, 36, 49, 64, 81, and 100 - the perfect squares. There are 10 such orbs in all.

<u>Final Answer:</u>

At the end of the Ritual of Turning, 10 orbs lie in rest, and 90 still shine, filling the forest with their quiet golden glow.

The Wizard's Trap (Puzzle VIII)

When the red door's illusion faded, the riddle became clear: Twenty-five horses. Only five can race at a time. No clocks. Find the top three, with certainty.

Since there were no timers, only the order of finishing could be used to decide who was faster. The key was to compare through reasoning, not by repeating the same races.

Step 1 - Five first races (R1–R5)
They divided the twenty-five steeds into five groups of five, marking them with symbols A, B, C, D, and E.
Each group ran once:
Race 1: A1 > A2 > A3 > A4 > A5
Race 2: B1 > B2 > B3 > B4 > B5
Race 3: C1 > C2 > C3 > C4 > C5
Race 4: D1 > D2 > D3 > D4 > D5
Race 5: E1 > E2 > E3 > E4 > E5
Five races revealed the best within each group.

Step 2 - Race of champions (R6)

They then raced the five group winners - A1, B1, C1, D1, and E1. Suppose the finishing order was:

A1 > B1 > C1 > D1 > E1

From this single race, Tiara deduced:

A1 is the fastest of all

(it beat every other group's winner).

At this point (after 6 races), the fastest horse overall is known: A1.

Step 3 - Narrowing the contenders for 2nd and 3rd

Tiara studied the list. "To find the next two, we don't need to test everyone again - only those who could still win a place."

Teksh nodded and listed them out:

- From Group A: A2 and A3 - they might be just behind A1.
- From Group B: B1 and B2 - since B1 lost only to A1, both B1 and B2 could still outrun A2 or A3.
- From Group C: C1 - since C1 lost only to A1 and B1, it could still outrun A2 and B2 for the third place.

Thus, only five contenders remain:

A2, A3, B1, B2, C1.

Step 4 - Final race (R7)

One final race among these five decides the remaining places.

Whoever finishes 1st in this final race is the second-fastest overall, and whoever finishes 2nd in this final race is the third-fastest overall (since A1 is already known to be fastest).

After this seventh race, Tiara can name the top three with complete certainty.

Final Answer:

- 5 races are needed so every horse runs once.
- 1 more to compare the group winners (find A1).
- 1 final to distinguish 2nd and 3rd among the only remaining possibilities.

Total – 7 races

The Desert of Dhatkidith (Puzzle IX)

The merchant has 3,000 sunfruits and one beast that can carry 1,000 at a time.

But the beast eats one fruit for every league it walks, whether it's going forward or coming back.

So, to carry fruits across the whole 1,000-league desert, the merchant must plan carefully.

He can't carry all 3,000 at once, so he'll make several trips - moving fruits in stages and leaving small piles (caches) along the way.

Explanation:

Stage 1: Too many fruits - 3,000

At first, he needs to move 3 loads (because 3,000 ÷ 1,000 = 3). That means for every league he goes forward, he must walk forward and back several times, which makes the beast eat 5 fruits per league. This is as shown:

2 forward (carrying load),

2 backward (partly loaded),

1 forward again (final delivery).

He keeps doing this until one full load (1,000 fruits) is eaten up in travel.

At 5 fruits per league, that happens after:

1000 ÷ 5 = 200 leagues.

After about 200 leagues, only 2,000 fruits are left to move.

<u>Stage 2: 2,000 fruits left</u>

Now, only 2 loads are left (2,000 ÷ 1,000 = 2)

For every league forward, the beast eats 3 fruits (since he's making fewer trips). This is as shown:

1 forward (carrying load),

1 backward (partly loaded),

1 forward again (final delivery).

He keeps doing this until one full load (1,000 fruits) is eaten up in travel.

At 3 fruits per league, that happens after:

1000 ÷ 3 = 333 leagues. *(Ignore fraction)*

After about 333 leagues, only 1,000 fruits are left to move.

Phase 3 - Final Journey

Now the beast can carry all 1,000 fruits at once. For the last part of the journey (about 467 leagues), the beast eats one fruit per league.

By the time he reaches the far market, he has about 533 fruits left.

Check Points:

- Phase 1: 200 × 5 = 1000 fruits eaten.
- Phase 2: 333 × 3 = 1000 fruits eaten.
- Phase 3: 467 × 1 = 467 fruits eaten.
- Remaining = 3000 − (1000 + 1000 + 467) = 533 fruits delivered.

Final Answer:

The merchant can deliver 533 sunfruits to the market.

The Temple of Light (Puzzle X)

- There are 100 guardians in the Temple of Light.
- Each can see every other guardian's flame but not their own.
- If a guardian ever becomes certain their own flame burns, they must extinguish it and leave at dawn.
- All departures are visible to all.
- One night, a lone wanderer publicly says:
  "At least one flame among you burns brightly."
- After this announcement, 'X' guardians left the temple together on a specific dawn.

Question:

When will the guardians leave, how many and why?

Answer in brief:

All 100 guardians will leave together at dawn on the 100th day after the wanderer's announcement.

No one leaves before that.

How the guardians think

Let's imagine it step by step:

If there was only 1 flame:

That guardian would look around and see no other lights. Hearing "at least one flame burns," they'd instantly realize,

"Then it must be mine."

They'd leave the next morning.

If there were 2 flames:

Each guardian would see 1 other light.

They'd think, "If I don't have a flame, that person sees no flames and will leave tomorrow."

When no one leaves the next morning, both realize,

"Oh - the other one must have seen my flame too."

So, both leave together on the second day.

If there were 3 flames:

Each sees two others burning.

They wait two days - expecting the pair to leave if there were only two flames.

When nobody leaves after two days, they realize,

"That means my flame must also be burning!"
All three leave together on the third day.

And so on...

<u>So, what happens in the temple?</u>

Each guardian counts the days, waiting for the pattern to reveal itself.
If there are 100 flames burning, they will all wait through 99 silent dawns.
When the 100th dawn comes and still no one has left, every guardian finally understands - their own flame must also burn.
So, all 100 guardians leave together on the 100th day.

<u>Why the wanderer's words mattered</u>

Before the wanderer spoke, everyone could *see* other flames, but no one *knew for sure that everyone else also knew it too.*

That one sentence created "shared knowing" - a chain of understanding that spread through every mind in the temple, setting off the countdown that led to their final, perfect harmony.

Final Answer:

All 100 guardians will extinguish their flames and depart at dawn on the 100th day after the wanderer's declaration.

The Architect of Paradox (Puzzle XI)

When Chantrik presented his question, Tiara realized it was not just a test of logic-it was a test of trust, patience, and order. One hundred souls, one chamber, one light. No speech, no sign, no second chance.

How could they prove that all had entered at least once, without ever meeting again?

She thought carefully. A single light could mean yes or no-but together, it could become something more: a signal.

---

(1) <u>Choose one leader - the Counter.</u>
Before the test begins, everyone agrees that one special person will keep count.
That's the Counter's only job.

(2) The others will send signals using the lamp.
The first time any normal soul enters and sees the lamp off, they will turn it on.
That means, "I've been here."

After that, they never touch the lamp again - not ever. If anyone enters, even for the first time, and finds the lamp already on, they simply leave it as it is..

(3) The Counter collects the signals.

Every time the Counter enters and finds the lamp on, he turns it off and adds 1 to his count.

He never turns it on himself.

(4) The pattern continues.

Each new "ON" means one new person has entered for the first time.

Each "OFF" by the Counter means he's counted that visit.

(5) When the Counter's count reaches 99,

he knows every other soul has entered once - and that he himself, being inside already, is the hundredth. At that moment, he can declare with confidence:

"All 100 souls have entered."

Final Answer:

Only one person (the Counter) ever turns the lamp off. Everyone else turns it on only once.

That way, each "on" the Counter finds represents a new person. Eventually, the Counter gathers all 99 signals, one by one.

It might take a long time, but it's foolproof - no guessing, no mistakes.

Author's Note

This book is born from my lifelong love for solving puzzles. Since my daughter, Shanaya (Tia), was four years old, I have been sharing imaginary stories with her - stories that always carried a hidden puzzle within. Over time, I watched how these small challenges strengthened her curiosity, logic, and problem-solving abilities in wonderful ways.

That experience made me realize that puzzles are more than games - they are tools that train the mind to think clearly and creatively. They can help children and young adults develop a way of reasoning that blends imagination with intelligence.

With that belief, I've tried to create a new kind of storytelling - a genre I call "**PuzzTales**" - stories woven with puzzles. My hope is that Nautica: The Sapphire Cube becomes more than a fantasy adventure; that it inspires young readers to think, question, and discover the joy of solving the world around them.

Connect with Bhavuk:
Email id: puzztales.nautica@gmail.com
Instagram: @puzztales.nautica

Acknowledgments

To my family - my parents, my wife, and my loved ones - thank you for always giving me strength, wisdom, and support. Your faith made the impossible feel effortless and helped this dream come true. You stood by me in every moment, teaching me that patience and belief can turn imagination into reality.

To my daughter, Shanaya (Tia) - the heart and spark of Nautica. You listened, questioned, and explored every story and puzzle I shared, and in doing so, brought life to Tiara herself. Your curiosity and laughter made this journey far more magical than I ever imagined.

To my friends, mentors, and early supporters - your encouragement, insight, and belief helped this dream take form and find its rhythm.

And finally, to everyone who holds this book in their hands - may you carry its light forward. Because every story, like every river, flows farther when shared.

9 789355 252449

Printed at Repro India Ltd.